Lone Parents

ISSUES FOR THE NINETIES

Volume 8

Editor

Craig Donnellan

Independence

Educational Publishers
Cambridge

First published by Independence
PO Box 295
Cambridge CB1 3XP

British Library Cataloguing in Publication Data
Lone Parents – (Issues for the Nineties Series)
I. Donnellan, Craig II. Series
362.8294

ISBN 1 872995 73 X

Printed in Great Britain
at Leicester Printers Ltd
Leicester

Typeset by
Martyn Lusher Artwork, Cambridge

Cover
The illustration on the front cover is by
Anthony Haythornthwaite / Folio Collective.

CONTENTS

Introduction

Lone Parents is the eighth volume in the series: **Issues For The Nineties**. The aim of this series is to offer up-to-date information about important issues in our world.

Lone Parents examines the challenge facing lone parents, especially young single parents. The information comes from a wide variety of sources and includes:

Government reports and statistics
Newspaper reports and features
Magazine articles and surveys
Literature from lobby groups
and charitable organisations.

It is hoped that, as you read about the many aspects of the issues explored in this book, you will critically evaluate the information presented. It is important that you decide whether you are being presented with facts or opinions. Does the writer give a biased or an unbiased report? If an opinion is being expressed, do you agree with the writer?

Lone Parents offers a useful starting point for those who need convenient access to information about the many issues involved. However, it is only a starting point. At the back of the book is a list of organisations which you may want to contact for further information.

*****

Lone parenthood

A significant social change over the last 30 years has been the increase in the number of one-parent families as a result of the rise in divorce rates and the number of births outside marriage

As Figure 1 shows, Denmark has the highest proportion of lone parents in the European Union (one in five), followed by the UK (one in six). Greece, Spain and Italy have the lowest proportions, with around one in 20 families with dependent children being lone-parent families.

These national differences in the proportion of lone-parent families are related to the different routes into lone parenthood. Lone parents in the European Union can be grouped into four main categories: single, divorced, separated and widowed. In southern European countries, lone-parent families usually result from the death of one of the parents, whereas in other Member States they are the result of divorce, separation and extra-marital child-bearing.

For the European Union as a whole, the Eurobarometer survey found that around one in six lone parents are single, having never married or cohabited; all the rest have had a partner at some point. Three in ten are divorced or separated, whilst another three in ten are widowed (see Figure 2).

Lone parents are more likely to be in paid work than mothers in two-parent families in the European Union as a whole (60% compared with 54%). However, this masks marked national differences. Two groups emerge: those countries where fewer lone mothers are employed than couple mothers (UK, Ireland and the Netherlands) and those where the opposite is true (Southern Mediterranean countries, Germany and France).

This may be explained by factors such as the availability of childcare, different systems of benefits and support to lone-parent families.

Teenage pregnancies

The fertility rate amongst women under 20 years old has been decreasing in all European countries, except for the UK where it has increased slightly. The most notable decrease is found in Mediterranean countries and in Ireland, although they still have high rates. The highest rate of all is found in the UK, where 3% of all 15 to 19 year olds gave birth, which is more than three times as many as in the Netherlands or France (see Figure 3).

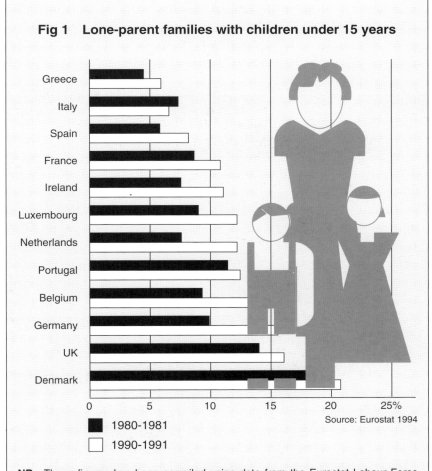

Fig 1   Lone-parent families with children under 15 years

■ 1980-1981
□ 1990-1991

Source: Eurostat 1994

NB These figures has been compiled using data from the Eurostat Labour Force Survey. However, there are variations between the current estimates of the number of lone parents in the European Union.

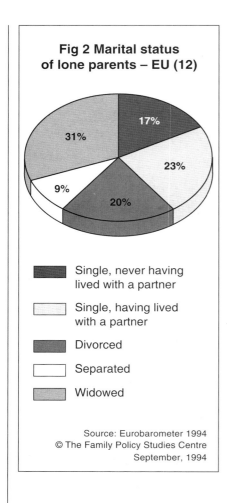

Fig 2 Marital status of lone parents – EU (12)

17%
23%
20%
9%
31%

■ Single, never having lived with a partner

□ Single, having lived with a partner

■ Divorced

□ Separated

■ Widowed

Source: Eurobarometer 1994
© The Family Policy Studies Centre
September, 1994

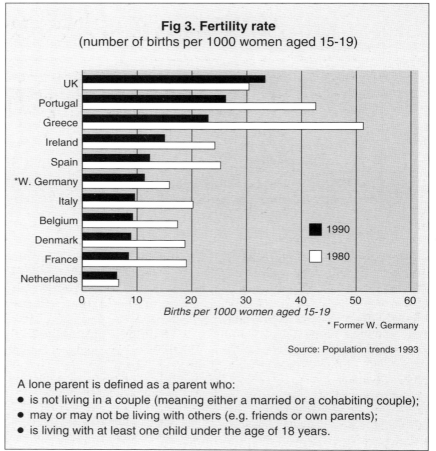

Fig 3. Fertility rate
(number of births per 1000 women aged 15-19)

UK
Portugal
Greece
Ireland
Spain
*W. Germany
Italy
Belgium
Denmark
France
Netherlands

■ 1990
□ 1980

Births per 1000 women aged 15-19

0   10   20   30   40   50   60

* Former W. Germany

Source: Population trends 1993

A lone parent is defined as a parent who:
- is not living in a couple (meaning either a married or a cohabiting couple);
- may or may not be living with others (e.g. friends or own parents);
- is living with at least one child under the age of 18 years.

From: Families in the European Union – Special Edition
*Available from The Family Policy Studies Centre
See page 39 for address details.*

See page 39 for address details.

Lone mothers in Britain

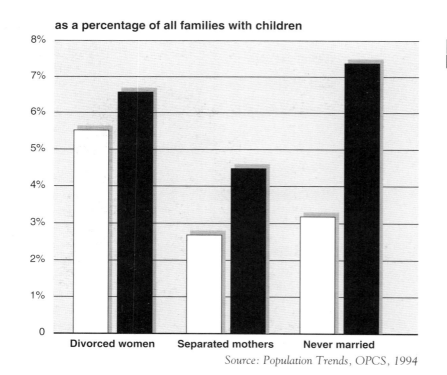

as a percentage of all families with children

□ 1986
■ 1992

8%
7%
6%
5%
4%
3%
2%
1%
0

Divorced women   Separated mothers   Never married

Source: Population Trends, OPCS, 1994

One in five families with children is a one-parent family, and never-married mothers are now the largest group of lone parents.

Around the world

Here we take a look at the position of one-parent families in Japan, America and Australia. Not surprisingly, many problems are the same the world over.

Japan

Unmarried mothers in Asahi, Japan are organised in a group to fight for rights they say are often denied them.

'While I was on maternity leave, a personnel division official came to my home and asked me to leave the company', said a 31-year-old member of the Unmarried Mothers' Society. She said that the father of her child, a colleague at her company, is married and has children.

'I didn't know what to do', she said, 'when he refused to pay for bringing up the baby.' The man, who does not want his family to know about the affair, escaped the heat by taking an overseas post.

The woman, who said she was mentally exhausted by her predicament, was able to bounce back after joining a group that evolved in the Unmarried Mothers' Society. 'Members helped me to wipe out a sense of guilt,' she said.

The group was first formed in 1984 when the government tried to reduce subsidies to unmarried mothers.

A 35-year-old member said she visited 30 to 40 real estate agents without being able to find an apartment that allows an unmarried mother with children. The unwed mothers' association helped her to find a place to live.

The above account from the *Asahi Evening Times* makes lone-parent issues in Japan appear very familiar. The figures make depressing reading. According to a 1988 Ministry of Health and Welfare study, single mother households (83% of all single parent households) had an average income of two million Yen in 1987, less than half the income of a two-parent family.

When the income of widows is excluded, this figure sunk to 1.9 million Yen. The majority of one-

By Sue Robertson

parent families are therefore living below the poverty line.

Welfare support is geared to help only the poorest families, and the Ministry of Health and Welfare does its best to discourage applications. Unwed mothers have it worst. An unwed mother cannot get state aid for dependent children at all if the child's father has admitted paternity, and welfare officers may use a letter or visit from a father as grounds for cutting off aid. Only 14% of divorced women receive maintenance from their ex-husbands.

This bleak scenario keeps the Japanese divorce rate low and the number of single mother households at only 2.2 per cent of all households. Discrimination against single mothers in areas such as housing and employment is very common, and groups like the one in Asahi have been formed to combat such prejudice and offer mutual support. They

have just launched a book *'Here's to single mothers'*, with chapter titles such as 'Thank goodness I got divorced' and 'Let's take advantage of the bureaucratic system'.

Two members of the Single Mothers' Forum in Japan will be attending the United Nations Non-Governmental Organisation Forum in Beijing and will be holding a workshop on single mothers. They are keen to make contact with other Single-Parent organisations, even if they cannot come to Beijing. Their address is:
Single Mothers' Forum,
3-23-2-204 minamityou tanasi-si, Tokyo, Japan. (Fax: 0424 66 9022)

North America

Sixteen million children in the US are poor – three times more than in Britain. The American taxpayer is tired of doling out billions of dollars in aid to the poor. Many see the ultimate symbol of the 'sponger' as the teenage mother trapped in a cycle of dependency on welfare. Under the existing federal aid programme,

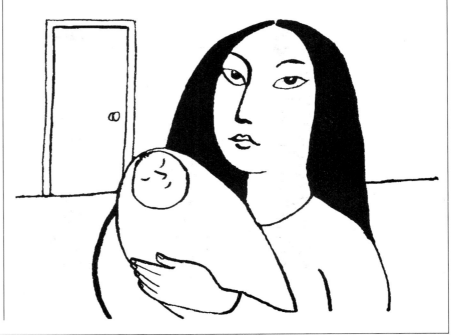

In the US, divorce accounts for 46% of single parent households

the more children a woman has, the bigger her welfare cheque.

All that is about to change. Politicians have jumped on the bandwagon and are all too eager to use the statistics to explain the creation of a 'social underclass' which has become dependent on the benefits system.

No one is disputing that the definition of the family is changing: it is whether that change poses a threat to society which seems to be the crux of the issue. Researchers are wary of attaching value judgements to their findings, and there is no clear evidence that children from the traditional two-parent family fare any better than children from any other circumstances.

Newt Gingrich, the Republican House Speaker, thinks that he has found the answer to America's welfare problem! Under the new 'Personal Responsibility Act' passed by the House in March, Republicans will ban welfare to underage mothers and prohibit the use of Federal money to pay for additional welfare benefits for children born to a family already receiving assistance under the Federal Aid to Families with Dependent Children programme.

The Senate has yet to debate this proposal. However, some States have already passed similar laws for their own welfare programmes, including New Jersey, Arkansas, Georgia, Indiana, Wisconsin and Nebraska.

Statistics

- Only 50% of American children live in a traditional nuclear family with married parents.

- Of the 66 million non-nuclear family children:
  24% live in single-parent families
  15% live in step families
  5.7% live with several generations
  3.5% live in households with non-relatives and many others combine more than one of these living situations.

- Divorce accounts for 46% of single parent households.

- Marital separation accounts for 21% of single parent households.

- Death of spouse accounts for 7% of single parent households.

Australia

In March this year I visited Australia. While there I took the chance to meet up with some Australian women to discuss feminist issues across the globe, which was extremely interesting and may just have some lessons for us here in Scotland.

At a Federal level, Australia currently has a Labour government, whereas at State level, almost every, state is Liberal (Conservative). This means that there is a rather mixed bag of ideas around.

On the progressive side, the Federal government seemed to have made good use of the International Year of the Family and had set up a working party which produced a major report with wide recommendations on making policies more family friendly.

Interestingly, their definition of the family was an inclusive one, encompassing all families including gay families, and the report recommended that the law be amended to remove discrimination against such families. This has been followed up at State level in some areas with the establishment of Offices of the Family. This had been done in South Australia by a Conservative government, yet the Office had the same inclusive approach to families.

One of their roles was to require a 'family audit' of all state policies to clarify their effect on families and also to analyse the cumulative effects of different policies by putting these audits together. One advantage of this approach was that issues such as childcare and family-friendly policies could be pursued as family issues rather than women's issues.

The Office were also aiming to line up influential figures in public life (sports, church etc.) who would be prepared to speak up in favour of the less conventional families such as lone parents, since Australian lone parents seem to be just as much a favourite scapegoat as in Britain.

Women's Offices had also been established at Federal and State level, and in several cases they had established Women's Information and Referral Exchange Services which acted as a central contact point for a wide range of women's organisations. Childcare seemed to be quite a lot better than in Britain with wide availability of pre-school and after-school care and two systems of subsidy, one for low income families and one on a universal basis for all families.

Not surprisingly, the latter was being questioned while I was there as being 'too expensive'. Child Support was also better, with an estimated 50-60% of parents eligible to receive payments under the new system actually doing so. That may not be unconnected with the fact that all parents keep part of child support payments, and that collection is through the tax system. However, just as over here, there have been massive protests by fathers and the government were about to implement reforms geared much more to fathers than to caring parents.

Less encouragingly, the Liberal Governments seemed to be importing conservative ideas from Britain and the United States at a depressing rate. Public expenditure was under attack, networks of Women's health centres in Victoria were being merged with the main stream health service, educational expenditure was being cut, with support services rapidly disappearing and the South Australian Government was discussing hiring English Accountants to run its schools. Already, so-called free education seemed to be a thing of the past with a system of 'voluntary' and compulsory school fees levied for

books, use of libraries and sports equipment.

Single parents I met talked of not being able to afford the fees and their children being excluded from gym lessons and being ostracised in the playground. Public housing was also in short supply, with many parents forced into the high rent private sector. This seemed to lead to quite a lot of house sharing, which then exposed lone parents to threats of being seen as cohabiting, with the Australian DSS reviewing lone-parent pensioners every 12 weeks to check they are not in a live-in relationship.

It also meant that parents were left in a poverty trap just as they are here. While the Job, Employment and Training scheme was welcomed, it was only seen as a partial success, not well enough resourced, and offering too low a level of training to allow escape from the poverty trap. Water privatisation was also on the political agenda.

Australia has an organisation called the Women's Electoral Lobby. WEL was set up in 1972, launching itself with a questionnaire on women's issues to all candidates for the Federal Government elections, the results of which were widely publicised.

Since then it has continued to lobby politicians at State and Federal level, and has built up a wide network of members, many of whom are in influential positions. Members give

each other support and campaign on specific issues such as women and employment, rural women, women and health and women in the media. They also run discussion days to inform their members on current issues.

Lone parents were represented by a number of organisations, including Councils for Single Mothers in Melbourne and Adelaide and a Lone Parent Support project in Sydney. These agencies had just got together at a national level, and had secured funding for one part-time worker nationally. However, at State level, they were better resourced with a number of paid staff and, in Melbourne's case, a regular slot on their Community Radio station.

Living standards compared

An Australian lone parent with two children aged 10 and 13 would be about £31 per week better off in benefit payments, compared with a lone parent in Britain.

In addition, she could earn up to £34 weekly before her benefit was reduced, and even then she would only lose 50p in the pound. Similarly, she could keep up to £11 per week maintenance without deduction from her benefit, and only lose half the payments above that.

Australian lone parents also get travel concessions and a telephone allowance of £6.80 per quarter and receive a training allowance of £15 per week if taking an approved training course.

Childcare assistance is also available, and an employment entry payment of £50 annually or an education entry payment of £100 annually is made if jobs or education are taken up.

These measures are part of a system that aims to make the transition between benefit and employment easier for lone parents. By contrast, the welfare benefit and child maintenance systems in Britain pose a series of barriers to those trying to escape from dependence on the State. The introduction of the Childcare Disregard on Family Credit and the proposed Maintenance Credits are slight improvements, but they are still not nearly enough.

© One-parent Families in Scotland
May, 1995

National Council for One Parent Families

Current facts and figures

The debate about the modern family and the increase in the number of one-parent families continued throughout 1993 and into 1994. The debate was fuelled by figures showing an increase in the numbers of people having children outside marriage and the steady rise in the number of lone parents relying on the welfare state.

All too often, however, these statistics were moulded to suit the purposes of those attempting to spread gloom about the breakdown of the family and the spiralling welfare bill for single parents. The National Council for One Parent Families challenged this distorted presentation of the facts and led the call for a sensible debate about the issues thrown up by the growth in one-parent families. In particular, we challenged the myth that the average lone parent is a feckless teenager who has deliberately become pregnant to get a council house and state benefits.

We have been at pains to point out that, far from gleefully milking the state, surveys show that the vast majority of lone parents want to become financially independent by taking a paid job which will increase their family income.

Numbers of lone parents

In 1992, 21 per cent of all families with dependent children in Great Britain were headed by a lone parent, i.e. one in five families. Between one in five and one in six dependent children were living in a one-parent family, approximately 90 per cent of which were headed by lone mothers.

Family types in 1992

The proportion of families headed by a lone parent rose from 8 per cent in 1971 to 21 per cent in 1992. This was due to an increase in families headed by a single, divorced or separated mother. Despite the impression often given in the media, 73 per cent of one-parent families result from divorce, separation or death. Only just over a third of lone mothers are single (i.e. never married). Only one-fifth of lone parents in Britain were under 25.

Live births outside marriage

The number of births outside marriage continues to rise and has more than doubled over the past decade. In 1992, births outside marriage were 31.2 per cent of all live births, compared to 30.2 per cent in 1991 and 14.4 per cent in 1982.

Again in contradiction to the impression given in response to these statistics, the number of births to teenage mums actually declined significantly in 1992. The number of births to unmarried teenagers dropped by 5 per cent to 31.7 births per 1,000 women from the previous recent high of 33.3 in 1990.

The vast majority of births outside marriage are registered by both parents, indicating that more people are choosing to have children without getting married rather than choosing to have children alone as is suggested by some commentators. Of the 40,000 live births outside marriage to teenagers, the vast majority, i.e. nearly 27,000, were registered by both parents. Overall, out of 215,225 births outside marriage, 163,753 were registered by two parents.

Social Security and financial resources

In August 1993 there were 1,040,000 lone parents claiming Income Support.

In 1992, nearly half of lone mothers got an income of less than £100 per week compared with only 4 per cent of married couples, while the number of lone parents getting over £350 was 11 per cent compared with 59 per cent of married couples. Lone fathers were likely to be better off than lone mums, with only 23 per cent getting less than £100 per week.

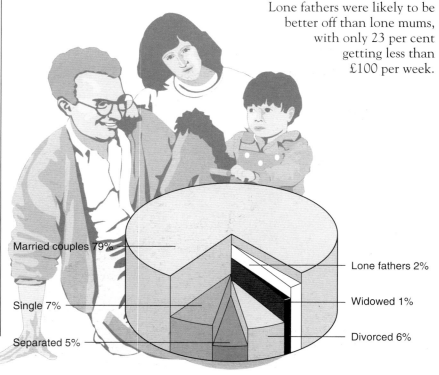

Married couples 79%

Single 7%

Separated 5%

Lone fathers 2%

Widowed 1%

Divorced 6%

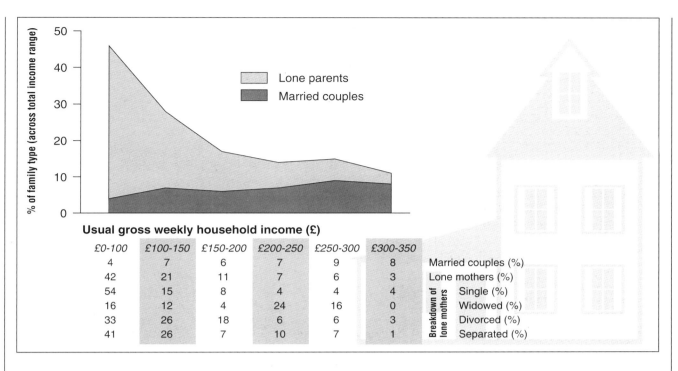

% of family type (across total income range)

Legend: Lone parents / Married couples

Usual gross weekly household income (£)

	£0-100	£100-150	£150-200	£200-250	£250-300	£300-350	
	4	7	6	7	9	8	Married couples (%)
	42	21	11	7	6	3	Lone mothers (%)
Breakdown of lone mothers	54	15	8	4	4	4	Single (%)
	16	12	4	24	16	0	Widowed (%)
	33	26	18	6	6	3	Divorced (%)
	41	26	7	10	7	1	Separated (%)

Employment

While the numbers of women working has increased steadily over the past ten years, the trend for lone parents is in the opposite direction. In 1992, 17 per cent of lone mothers with dependent children worked full-time and 24 per cent worked part-time.

According to a recent survey, *Lone parents and work*, published by the DSS, only 9 per cent of lone parents with a child under five worked full-time. Whilst most of the lone parents surveyed expressed a desire to work at some stage, many cited the lack of affordable childcare and the 'benefits trap' as key obstacles to getting a job.

Housing

Lone parents were more likely than other families to live in local authority housing and less likely to be owner occupiers. Only 29 per cent of lone parents had a mortgage compared to 70 per cent of other families.

While it has been claimed that single parents walk into the best council houses, the evidence is the opposite. Research carried out by the Institute of Housing in 1992 shows that there is a tendency to offer to one-parent families smaller-sized properties than to two-parent families. Nearly one-fifth of local authorities would require a lone mother and her child to share a bedroom.

Lone parents share same moral values

In March 1994 Sainsbury's published the findings of a major new survey on the modern family. The survey, which interviewed 14,000 people, showed that lone parents shared the same moral values and sense of parental responsibility as other parents. Eighty-nine per cent of lone parents said they thought parents should be responsible for their children up to the age of 16, and 72 per cent thought parents should be fined for crimes committed by their children.

Not surprisingly, lone parents reported more financial difficulties than other parents, and the survey showed that, while only a third of lone parents get away on holiday once a year, one in five never takes a holiday.

Key facts

Numbers

In 1992 there were 1.4 million one-parent families in Great Britain with 2.2 million children living in them. This means that 21 per cent of all families with dependent children are now headed by a lone parent.
(*Population Trends 78*, 1994)

Age and marital status

The majority of lone mothers, over 60 per cent, are married women who have separated, divorced or are widowed. Meanwhile, the largest single group of lone parents is now the single, never married lone parent.

The average age of the single lone parent has risen since 1988. Despite the impression often given that

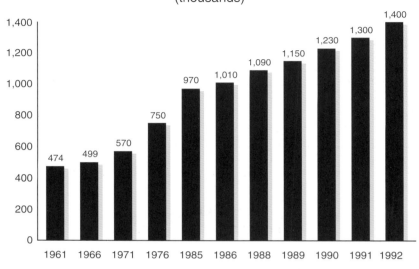

Numbers of one-parent families in Great Britain
(thousands)

- 1961: 474
- 1966: 499
- 1971: 570
- 1976: 750
- 1985: 970
- 1986: 1,010
- 1988: 1,090
- 1989: 1,150
- 1990: 1,230
- 1991: 1,300
- 1992: 1,400

(*Population Trends* 78, 1994)

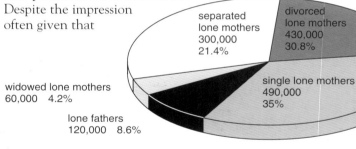

- separated lone mothers 300,000 21.4%
- divorced lone mothers 430,000 30.8%
- widowed lone mothers 60,000 4.2%
- lone fathers 120,000 8.6%
- single lone mothers 490,000 35%

large numbers of lone parents are feckless young teenagers, less than 4 per cent of all lone mothers were under 20. Meanwhile, almost 40 per cent were in their 20s.

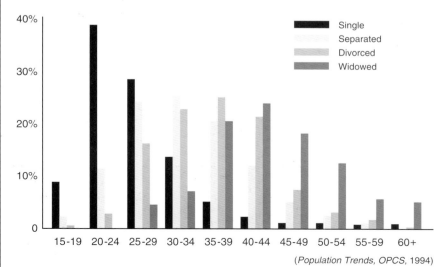

Proportions of lone mothers in the different age groups, by marital status, 1986-92 in Great Britain

Legend:
- Single
- Separated
- Divorced
- Widowed

Age groups: 15-19, 20-24, 25-29, 30-34, 35-39, 40-44, 45-49, 50-54, 55-59, 60+

(*Population Trends, OPCS*, 1994)

Lone fathers made up less than 9 per cent of all lone parents in 1992. Lone fathers tended to be older than lone mothers, with the largest proportion of lone fathers being in their early 40s compared to the largest proportion of lone mothers who were in their late 20s.

(*Population Trends 78*, 1994)

Children

One in five children lived in a one-parent family in 1992. The average number of children in one-parent families has been smaller than in families headed by a married or cohabiting couple. In 1992, families headed by a lone parent had on average 1.7 children, married couples had 1.9 children.

While nearly 20 per cent of the lone mothers who had been married had three or more children, only 7 per cent of single lone mothers had three or more children.

(General Household Survey 1992)

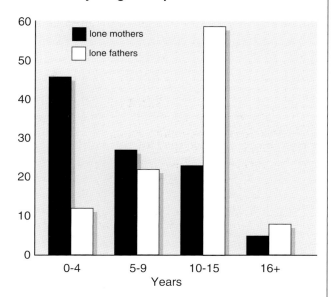

Percentage of lone mother and lone father families in Great Britain by age of youngest dependent child

Number of dependent children of lone mothers in Great Britain

one child 55%

two children 30%

three children 11%

four or more children 3%

(General Household Survey 1990, table 2.30)

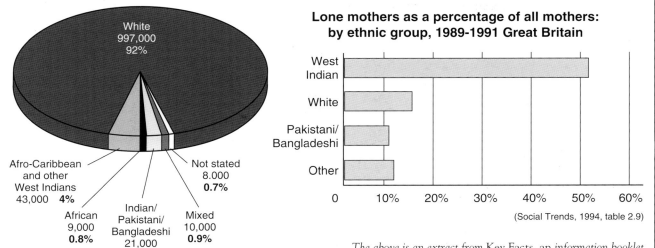

Ethnic origin

Ninety-two per cent of all lone parents are white. Just over one in ten Pakistani/Bangladeshi families are headed by a lone mother. Over half the mothers in the West Indian ethnic group were lone mothers in 1989-1991.

Estimated numbers of one-parent families by ethnic origin 1987/89 Great Britain

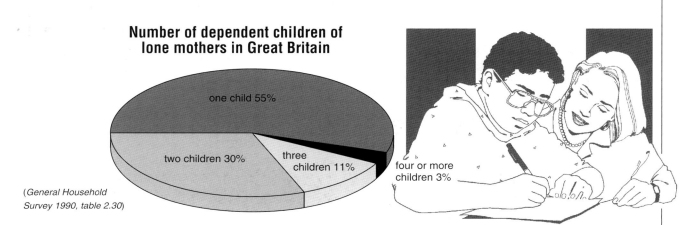

White 997,000 92%

Afro-Caribbean and other West Indians 43,000 **4%**

African 9,000 **0.8%**

Indian/ Pakistani/ Bangladeshi 21,000 **1.9%**

Mixed 10,000 **0.9%**

Not stated 8.000 **0.7%**

All ethnic groups 1,090,000   *(Population Trends 65, p38)*

Lone mothers as a percentage of all mothers: by ethnic group, 1989-1991 Great Britain

West Indian

White

Pakistani/ Bangladeshi

Other

0   10%   20%   30%   40%   50%   60%

(Social Trends, 1994, table 2.9)

The above is an extract from Key Facts, *an information booklet produced by The National Council for One Parent Families March, 1995*

When the cupboard is bare

An extract from *Nutrition and diet in lone parent families* by Elizabeth Dowler and Claire Calvert

> *I buy apples and bananas every fortnight. It's horrible when she has a banana and then says, 'Can I have an apple?' and you've got to stop her because it's got to last.*
>
> LONE MOTHER, MID-20S, CLAIMING INCOME SUPPORT, WITH ONE YOUNG DAUGHTER

Lone parents often live for long periods on income support, many with regular deductions being made and, until recently, no-one knew much about whether their or their children's food intakes suffered as a result.

For this study, supported by the Joseph Rowntree Foundation, we contacted about 200 lone parents in London through the DSS, and managed to persuade most of them to weigh and measure everything they and their family members ate for three days. Children took part, and often kept their own records, particularly about what they ate at school.

We used these records to estimate the actual nutrients people had eaten, and compared them to the Department of Health's reference values. We also interviewed the parents about the family's food patterns, where they bought food and why, and how they managed their budgets, particularly in terms of food.

The good news is that, in spite of their circumstances, lone parents who aim to shop for and cook healthy, fresh food achieve better diets for themselves and their children. This is true even where the parents smoke. Also, those who shop for and eat diets that are typical of black British or Afro-Caribbean lone parent families by and large do better nutritionally than those eating meals typical of white families.

Nevertheless, despite any positive approach, the diets of poorer families were still less healthy than those of better-off families. School meals were important for the intakes of children whose parents claimed income support, although many were unhappy

> *He gets hot nourishing food inside him – he gets meat I can't afford to buy; veg I can't afford to buy; he gets a pudding. If I did a sandwich I'd have to put jam on it. School holidays are a nightmare; trying to give him that extra meal a day is impossible.*
>
> LONE MOTHER, EARLY 40S, CLAIMING INCOME SUPPORT, REFERRING TO SON HAVING FREE SCHOOL MEALS

> *The kids can't just come in and help themselves to food. They don't have access to milk just to drink, milk goes on their cereal. Their hot chocolate at night is mostly water.*
>
> LONE MOTHER, MID-30S, CLAIMING INCOME SUPPORT, WITH TWO TEENAGERS

at the limited choices on offer – and what might happen in the future with school budget cuts.

The bad news is that those who had been unemployed for more than a year, lived in rented or local authority housing and took no holidays, had much worse diets than those not in these circumstances. This was particularly so if they also had money taken from their benefit to pay off debts and arrears, or paid their fuel bills through a key meter. Benefits don't go very far at the best of times, but if money is being taken off regularly, something has to give, and it usually seems to be food.

A lot of people said they tried not to cut back on food – they would delay paying rent or fuel bills, or would borrow from their family, rather than have nothing but bread or rice to eat. But even so, the reality was that they didn't buy much fruit, and ate less meat or fish than they

would like. People in these circumstances ate fewer fruits and vegetables, and tended to eat more biscuits, cakes, crisps, fatty processed meats – things that fill you up cheaply because they contain a lot of fat and few vitamins and minerals.

The second piece of bad news is that the ways in which people tried to cope with limited money also led to poorer nutrition outcomes. Lone parents who were the most financially stressed often bought stamps to pay for future bills, or used key meters, or bought goods and clothes through catalogues. These strategies were seen as good because they prevented people getting into debt or arrears again. However, these parents had poorer diets and nutrient intakes than those who didn't need

to use these controlling strategies, or at the time of the survey had chosen not to use them.

The poorest parents who only bought food in discount stores also had lower nutrient intakes and worse dietary patterns than parents who bought food in markets and supermarkets as well or instead. The range of food in discount stores may be limited, but it's the amount to spend on food that counts most. Other than that, where people shopped for food, and how they used their store cupboard and fridge/freezers, seemed to make little difference.

The mixed blessing news was that lone parents seem to protect their children: where there is evidence of nutritional deprivation, it is the parents who tend to suffer it.

● *Nutrition and diet in lone parent families* by Elizabeth Dowler and Claire Calvert is available from the Family Policies Studies Centre, price £9.50 + £1.50 p & p. See page 39 for address details. Elizabeth Dowler is at the Centre for Human Nutrition at the London School of Hygiene and Tropical Medicine.

Poverty for children as parents go it alone

By David Hughes
Political Editor

The number of lone parents is soaring and with it the number of children living in poverty, according to researchers.

Of 3.7 million youngsters below the poverty line, 1.8 million live with a single parent, according to a report commissioned by the Commons Social Security Select Committee.

Behind the new trend is a sharp increase in the number of parents who have never been married and are dependent on income support – up from 320,000 in 1989 to 440,000 in 1992. Lone parenthood had overtaken unemployment as the biggest source of poverty, said committee chairman Frank Field, calling for a major Government policy switch. Ministers could no longer assume that reducing unemployment would lead to reduced welfare spending.

The trend was for young single women to have children by young men who were permanently unemployed.

Government failure to provide training places for 900,000 young men was partly to blame. 'If they cannot get a job, they drift,' went on Mr Field, Labour MP for Birkenhead.

'They are without money and not very marriageable. This reinforces the trend of younger women thinking it's better to make it on their own.'

The research, conducted for the committee by the Institute of Fiscal Studies, reveals that as many as a quarter of a million young men are

Lone parenthood has overtaken unemployment as the biggest source of poverty

living with their parents without rights to any benefit.

Some were being pushed into 'prolonged adolescence', Mr Field declared.

Malcolm Wicks, Labour MP for Croydon North-West, said it was appalling that 3.7 million youngsters were in poverty. 'This is an extraordinarily large number of children living in grim circumstances in Britain at a time when, at the top, we have evidence that directors of privatised utilities are paying themselves Monopoly money.'

But Peter Thurnham, Tory MP for Bolton North-East, insisted that the figures should be taken in context.

Of the 'poorest' 10 per cent of the population, 86 per cent had a washing machine, 65 per cent had a video recorder and 53 per cent a car or van.

Are you missing out on £300 a year?

Almost half a million lone parents are missing out on £300 a year because of unclaimed one-parent benefit, explains Anthony Bailey

One parent benefit is an extra payment on top of Child Benefit available to parents who bring children up on their own. One reason many fail to claim is because they receive Income Support.

For these the extra benefit is deducted from Income Support, leaving them no better off. But many working lone parents could be missing out on £6.15 a week.

'I started back at work last May and always claimed One-parent benefit, even when I was on income support,' says Kerry Paine, 29, from Berkshire. Kerry has a seven-year-old son, Thys, and a four-year-old daughter, Maya.

Her family helps out with the children which means Kerry can work full-time at the Patrick McGrath staff library in Broadmoor Hospital.

'Having a job has made me much more contented. I hated living off Income Support and never had any money for those little treats for the children,' says Kerry.

It is a sentiment which strikes a chord at the National Council For One Parent Families. 'Many lone parents want to get back to work. In fact, our major priority is to lobby government to make this easier,' says NCFOPF's Fiona Fox.

'We think One-parent Benefit is important because it is not means-tested. It can make a difference when you are calculating whether you will be better off by getting a job.

'We would encourage people on Income Support to put in a claim. It helps them get out of the benefit trap where they are better off on Income Support,' says Fiona.

'But people should tread carefully if they are near the Income Support borderline,' says Fiona, 'For a small number of people, the extra benefit will take them off Income Support altogether.'

This means they could lose out on things like free prescriptions and free school dinners.

One-parent Benefit goes up to £6.30 a week on April 10. It is paid in addition to Child Benefit, currently £10.20 for the first child and £8.25 for other children (£10.40 and £8.45 from April 1995). The benefit is paid until a child reaches 16, or 19 if in full-time education up to A-level standard.

● For information, phone the Benefits Agency's Freeline on 0800 666 555.

© *Today*
January, 1995

One-parent Benefit

If you qualify for Child Benefit and you are bringing up a child on your own, you may also be able to get One-parent Benefit, a weekly payment. The amount paid is the same whatever your income or savings, or however many children you have. It is tax free.

Who can get One-parent Benefit?

You can get One-parent Benefit if:
● you can get Child Benefit and
● you are single, divorced, permanently separated, a widower or a widow (and you Widow's benefit does not include extra money for a child).

But you cannot get One-parent Benefit if:
● you are living with someone as husband and wife. Ask at your Social Security office for leaflet INF 3 *Living together as husband and wife* if you want to know how this applies to you.
● you and your partner are temporarily separated – for example, if one of you is in hospital, in prison or is abroad.
● you are already getting extra money for your eldest or only dependent child with one of the following benefits (this is because One-parent Benefit is paid for the eldest or only dependent child);
– Widowed Mother's Allowance
– War widow's pension
– Invalid Care Allowance
– State Retirement Pension
– Unemployability Supplement paid with Industrial Disablement Pension
– Industrial Death Benefit at the higher rate for a child (paid with an Industrial Injuries Widow's Pension).

If you get one of these benefits but are not sure whether it includes extra for your eldest or only dependent child, you can check with the office that deals with your benefit. If you make a claim. the Child Benefit Centre will check for you.

© *Department of Social Security*
August, 1994

Lone parent link to poverty triggers MPs' call for benefits reappraisal

By David Brindle
Social Services Correspondent

A committee of MPs yesterday urged a reappraisal of social security policy after figures showed that one in two children living in the poorest households is part of a lone-parent family.

Frank Field, chairman of the Commons social security select committee, said the figures proved that benefits spending was no longer largely cyclical and would not fall in line with declining unemployment.

'This is a massively important point which has yet to register on the political agenda,' Mr Field said. 'Before, you could expect falling unemployment to cut your welfare rolls, but there is now no automatic adjustment.'

The figures, commissioned by the committee, show that in 1992 there were almost 3.7 million children in families either dependent on safety-net income support benefit or having net resources below the level of the benefit.

Of the total, 1.8 million were children of lone parents.

The statistics also show that the number of lone parents not in full-time work and claiming income support rose from 2.1 million in 1989 to 2.7 million in 1992, including an increase from 32,000 to 440,000 in lone parents who never married.

Although strenuous efforts are being made to encourage lone parents to re-enter the labour market, the overwhelming majority rely on benefit. The committee is pressing the Government to conduct urgent research into how long people remain on benefit and how and why they come off it.

The data, prepared by the independent Institute for Fiscal Studies at a cost to the committee of £15,000 continue a 'low-income families' statistical series ended by the Department of Social Security when it introduced alternative figures for households below average income.

Among the institute's findings is that up to 250,000 unemployed, young men are living with their parents without any earnings or right to benefit until age 18.

Mr Field said: 'What we have got for some young males now is that we are pushing them into a period of prolonged adolescence. They are not getting benefit and the only thing is to drift.'

Malcolm Wicks, Labour MP for Croydon North-West and a former director of the Family Policy Studies Centre, said it was appalling that 3.7 million children should be in poverty.

'This is an extraordinarily large number of children living in grim circumstances in Britain at a time when, at the top, we have evidence that directors of privatised utilities are paying themselves Monopoly money,' Mr Wicks said.

However, Peter Thurnham, Conservative MP for Bolton North-East, said the figures had to be set in context.

Taking the poorest tenth of the population by income after allowing for housing costs, 86 per cent had a washing machine, 65 per cent a video recorder and 53 per cent a car or van, he said.

Alistair Burt, junior social security minister, said in the Commons on Monday that half the households reporting nil or negative incomes – many of them self-employed – spent more than the average for the population as a whole.

© The Guardian
March, 1995

Children in poverty

Estimated numbers of children in families dependent on Income Support or in families whose resources are below the level of Income Support although they do not meet the criteria to receive it. Great Britain, 1992, thousands, by type of family.

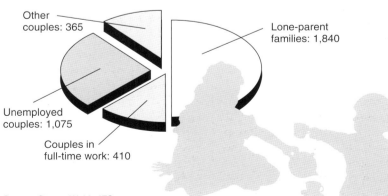

Other couples: 365

Lone-parent families: 1,840

Unemployed couples: 1,075

Couples in full-time work: 410

Source: Steven Webb, IFS
Low income statistics: low income families 1989-1992; HMSO; £8.95

Lone parents' income

Gross normal weekly disposable income (£s) inclusive of Housing Benefit

In 1992 the gross weekly income of one-parent families was 38.2 per cent of two-parent families with two children. Forty-two per cent of lone mothers lived on less than £100 per week, compared to only 4 per cent of married couples. In stark contrast, nearly 60 per cent of married couples had a gross weekly income of more than £350 compared to only 11 per cent of lone mothers.

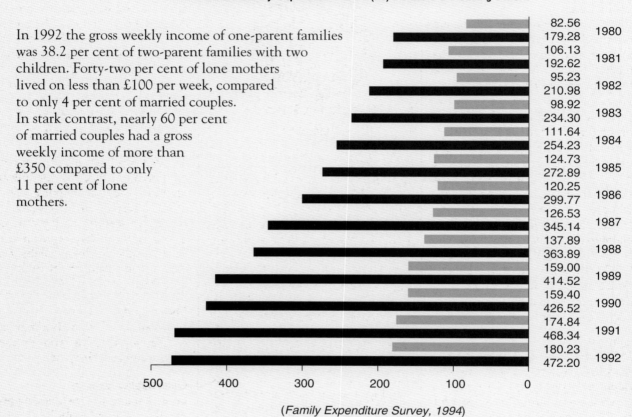

82.56	1980
179.28	1980
106.13	1981
192.62	1981
95.23	1982
210.98	1982
98.92	1983
234.30	1983
111.64	1984
254.23	1984
124.73	1985
272.89	1985
120.25	1986
299.77	1986
126.53	1987
345.14	1987
137.89	1988
363.89	1988
159.00	1989
414.52	1989
159.40	1990
426.52	1990
174.84	1991
468.34	1991
180.23	1992
472.20	1992

500   400   300   200   100   0

(Family Expenditure Survey, 1994)

Usual gross weekly household income by family type

Usual gross weekly household income

Family type	£0.01–£100.00	£100.01–£150.00	£150.01–£200.00	£200.01–£250.00	£250.01–£300.00	£300.01–£350.00	£350.01 and over
	percentage						
married couple	4	7	6	7	9	8	59
lone mother	42	21	11	7	6	3	11
single	54	15	8	4	4	4	12
widowed	16	12	4	24	16	0	28
divorced	33	26	18	6	6	3	9
separated	41	26	7	10	7	1	9
lone father	23	10	12	10	10	8	8
all lone parents	40	20	11	7	6	3	12

(General Household Survey, 1994)

The above is an extract from Key Facts an information booklet available from The National Council for One Parent Families

On your own with a baby

Information from One Parent Families Scotland

Money

Under sixteen

If you are under 16 years old you are not entitled to claim Income Support in your own right. If your parents receive Income Support, they will be able to claim free milk and vitamins on your behalf once the pregnancy is confirmed. Also, a one-off Maternity Payment of £100 will be available from the Social Fund.

Once the baby is born, you will be entitled to claim Child Benefit (£10.40) and One-Parent Benefit (£6.30). If your parents receive Income Support, they may be able to claim extra Income Support for the baby, but they should check first. Child Benefit and One-Parent Benefit are counted as income and deducted from Income Support, so it could leave them worse off.

Over 16

If you are 18 years or over and not working, you can claim Income Support. If you are aged 16 or 17, you can only claim Income Support for the last 11 weeks of pregnancy, or if you have a child. If a pregnant 16/17 year old becomes unemployed or finishes a YT course, she is entitled to a Bridging Allowance of £15 per week for up to 8 weeks. Thereafter she may be entitled to claim Income Support under the severe hardship rule.

You will be able to claim the Maternity Payment of £100.

Once the baby is born you can claim Child Benefit (£10.40) and One-Parent Benefit (£6.30).

The Social Fund can also provide loans and grants to people in need. These are not a 'right' and only limited money is available.

Community Care Grants can help with setting up home, preventing a child going into care, easing exceptional pressure and travelling expenses. Loans can also be made to pay for essential items or 'one-off' expenses.

One Parent Families Scotland

Working

If you have worked for at least six months, you may qualify for Statutory Maternity Pay (SMP). Otherwise, if you have been recently employed, you may get Maternity Allowance from the DSS. If you are not entitled to Maternity Allowance but you worked in the last few years, you may be able to get Sickness Benefit.

Statutory Maternity Pay is paid to those employed for 6 months at 90% of earnings for the first 6 weeks and £52.50 weekly for 12 weeks. Maternity Allowance for those employed less than 6 months rises to £52.50 weekly. All women employees paying NI contributions will receive at least 14 weeks off paid at one of these rates.

If you continue to work once the baby is born, and you work for less than 16 hours a week, you may claim Income Support and keep £15 of your net earnings without this affecting your benefit. If you work 16 hours or more a week and have a low wage, you can apply to the DSS for Family Credit. The first £15 of maintenance is disregarded in the calculation (Family Credit payments may affect Housing Benefit – seek advice).

From July 1995, women who qualify for Family Credit and who work more than 30 hours per week will get an extra £10 Family Credit weekly.

Other benefits

If you are claiming either Income Support or Family Credit, or have a low wage, you should also claim housing benefit from the local authority housing department and council tax benefit. All pregnant women and mothers of babies under a year old are entitled to free pre-scriptions and dental treatment. All mothers on Income Support or Family Credit are entitled to free prescriptions and dental treatment, and also to free fares to hospital for treatment or visiting.

All mothers claiming Income Support are entitled to free milk and vitamins and free school meals for older children if they have them.

More details of benefits are given in the *Information for One-parent families* leaflet, available from One-Parent Families Scotland or One Plus.

Living together

If you start to live with a man as a couple, you may lose your personal right to Income Support.

Child Support Agency

Lone Parents on Income Support, Family Credit or Disability Working Allowance are required by the Child Support Agency to pursue mainten-ance. Refusal to authorise this may result in a Benefit Penalty unless there are reasonable grounds for believing that you or any child living with you would suffer 'harm or undue distress' (contact SCSP for advice leaflet).

If you are on Income Support, your benefit will be reduced by the full amount of any maintenance you receive. If you are on Family Credit, you are allowed to keep £15 mainten-ance before your benefit is reduced.

Housing

Finding housing is often a major problem for young mothers. The main options are likely to be:

Remaining at home: If you remain at home and want a Council House of your own in the future you should put your name down on the Housing Waiting List. You must be 16 years or over.

Homelessness: If your family will not let you stay with them or there is overcrowding, you will qualify as homeless. The Council must help if you are pregnant or have a child and you are 16 years or over.

Housing Associations: Some Housing Associations provide flats or houses for lone parents at reasonable rents. Other Housing Associations are open to anyone who meets their criteria. Apply direct or ask your Local Council to nominate you for a Housing Association property.

Supported Accommodation: Some Housing Associations and voluntary organisations provide accommodation where a Support Worker can offer practical support and advice (see page 39 for addresses).

Private Rented Housing: Is often available locally, furnished or unfurnished. A deposit or rent in advance is normally required.

Before giving up any tenancy – seek advice!

Health

Your own health is important for you and your child. Post-natal checks are available usually six weeks after the birth, either at the hospital or with your own doctor.

The health visitor attached to your doctor's practice will visit you and your baby at home. You should also take your baby to the local clinic.

You can have the baby weighed and immunised at the clinic or at your doctor's. If you have any worries about the baby's feeding, crying or other problems, do contact the health visitor. She may also be able to introduce you to other mothers on their own.

Having a baby to care for is a major change in anyone's life. The National Childbirth Trust and the Cry-sis Society will be able to provide more information and advice on a wide range of issues, e.g. breast-feeding, sleeping problems, etc. (Information is available from One-parent Families Scotland – address details on page 39).

Benefits

Out of 1.4 million one-parent families in Great Britain 1,048,000 (75 per cent) were in receipt of Income Support in May 1993.

228,000 lone parents (16 per cent) received Family Credit, an in-work benefit designed to top-up low-income families.

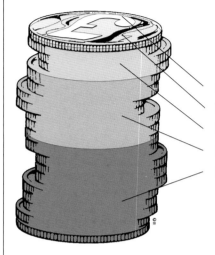

Lone mothers claiming Income Support by marital status in May 1993

Prisoners' partners	0.3%	3000
Widows	1.6%	16,000
Divorced women	19%	192,000
Separated women	31%	315,000
Single mothers	47%	464,000
Total		989,000

Source: Social Security Statistics 1994

Education and training

Women under 18 years

A teenage mother may still be at school when pregnant. In some areas, schools provide a support system for mothers. Home tuition schemes are also run by some Councils. School Careers Advisors should advise you on all the possibilities available. All unemployed 16/17 year olds are in theory guaranteed a place on Youth Training, even if pregnant. In practice, there is a shortage of places. However, even if available, some schemes are not suitable for pregnant women.

If a trainee has had to leave a course, she has the right to return and finish her training up to one year after she left to have the baby. Check with your local office for further details.

Women over 18 years

Knowing where to go for information on courses or training is often confusing.

Each Local Authority has a careers service which offers advice, information and guidance on further and higher education, careers and vocational training. There may or may not be a separate Adult Advisory Unit within your local careers service.

Advice and information for adults on vocational and non-vocational courses in local schools, community centres and colleges are often available from your local Community Education office/centre or the local college.

Job Centres will have information on government training schemes and schemes run by private and voluntary sectors (via TAP database). You may be able to do training and get payment of travel expenses and childcare costs.

Unfortunately, there are few childcare possibilities for young babies unless parents/relations can help.

● The above is an extract from a leaflet, *On your own with a baby*, published by One Parent Families, Scotland. Please see page 39 for address details.

© *One Parent Families, Scotland April, 1995*

The trials of a toddler with wanderlust

Jean Sandison, tells of the daily triumphs and tears of a single mother in the Highlands as she copes with a spirited daughter whose ambition is to lose herself

A single parent has to learn to live without luxuries. You don't think about them because it just makes you unhappy.

A sweater and a pair of jeans cost anything up to £60 these days, and where is a single mother going to find that kind of money?

After buying the necessities, I spend any cash I have on Jessica, my two year old daughter. But watching other women choose a new dress, or an attractive top in one of the inviting shops in the Eastgate Centre in Inverness where I live, can be depressing.

If I have only a few things to buy I let Jessica walk, which she always wants to do, because shopping with a push-chair is horrendous. We spend most of our time weaving in and out, dodging people, waiting for lifts, struggling with doors and over-loaded bags.

Life for a single parent is not just about having no money. Nor is it simply about a child without a father. It is also about all the other things couples take for granted: sharing daily tasks, baby-minding, dreaming dreams, planning for the future, and right down to opening doors and helping with the shopping.

And my little darling gets bored very quickly with shopping, and soon refuses point-blank to go into yet another shop.

I explain that mummy is not having much fun either, and that I would also rather be at home, doing much more interesting things. But to no avail. I recall one incident when I needed a pair of jeans. Every time I turned into the shop Jessica screamed wildly, shouting in protest. The sales assistant watched this performance for days until, finally, I arranged a baby-sitter and made a quick dash down town.

The assistant smiled knowingly and asked: 'And how is your little lady today?'

Mind you, it's an entirely different matter when Jessica decides it is toy-time, a fact I will remind her of when she is older and wants clothes for herself.

No matter what I plan, we invariably end up in the toy shop. But it is interesting to watch her with other children. Jessica is bossy – takes after her mother, I suppose – and it can be embarrassing. If anyone stands in the way of the push-chair, she yells at them 'move', or 'go away'.

If a child or baby is crying, Jessica tells them to 'shut up'. Mothers look at me admiringly and asks if I would like to do a 'swap'.

This is amusing and brightens shopping expeditions enormously – except when we go to Safeways. Because our flat is so small, the moment Jessica is confronted by wide-open spaces she is off like a shot. Most children choose a park, but not Jessica. She waits until Safeways.

I try to keep her in the trolley for as long as possible, but she crawls out and escapes before the second aisle. There are small trolleys at the check-outs in which hand baskets are stored. If Jessica spots an empty one she grabs it and is off full speed before I can mutter butter. I pretend I have no idea whose child she is and continue shopping.

I hear her calling: 'Jean, where are you?' all round the shop, until some poor old lady comes limping round the corner, quickly followed by the manager expressing grave concern about my daughter causing grievous bodily harm to customers. Nearby family parties 'tut tut' disapprovingly.

I rent a three-room flat in Inverness: bed-sit, kitchen and bathroom. Our home is in a convenient, quiet and friendly part of town. It is close to good shops, a medical centre, church and an excellent school which I hope, eventually, Jessica will attend.

But I was brought up in the country and have fond childhood memories. I want Jessica to share that experience and I dream of a cottage, a garden, a cat and some dogs, of course, a car. And, who knows, perhaps some day, even a husband. I want more – anybody in my position would.

Happily, Jessica and I can visit my friend, Fiona, who lives with her husband in a cottage at Hopeman on the Moray Firth, where we walk along the beach and occasionally hill hike.

We climbed Bad a'Churaich' (409m) by Lochindorb recently. Jessica wanted to walk alone, and, for once, could do so safely. Carrying her down was even nicer.

It was a big difference from going from street to street, shop to shop. That's not very exciting for a vibrant two year old. Nor, for that matter for her mother.

But at least we can come home to our own flat; which is a whole lot more than many single parents can, and I count myself very lucky indeed. And I have Jessica.

No matter what happens, at the end of the day, that is all that really matters.

© *The Herald*
March, 1995

Lone parents

Around 93% of lone parents are women and, while the number of women going out to work has increased in the last decade and a half, most of this has been amongst women who are either married or co-habiting. The numbers of lone mothers in the UK who are working has actually fallen from 49% in 1981 to 42% in 1991 according to figures from the *General Household Survey*, although working lone mothers work longer hours than other married or co-habiting women workers.

The biggest barriers to obtaining work are the poverty trap and lack of affordable childcare facilities. If this situation continues and lone parenthood continues to be more common, increasing numbers of children will fall into poverty.

- Around 93% of lone parents in the UK are women.
- Two-thirds of lone parent households are the result of divorce, separation and widowhood.
- Of the third of single parents who are lone mothers, many have lived with a partner. (*Population Trends 1993*, HMSO quoted in *Scottish Council for Single Parents Annual Report 1993/4 p2*)

The table below shows the gender bias in lone parenthood. Where there are children under 5 years of age in the household, it is headed by 97% of cases by a woman. Under 5s childcare is woefully inadequate in Scotland. Women's earnings also tend to be less than men's. Even when the lone mother can obtain work, the family could still be dependent on a very low income.

- Nearly two-thirds of lone-parents are economically inactive.
- Just over 30% are in employment and half of these are part-time workers.

The above is an extract from *Child and family poverty in Scotland – the facts*.

© *Glasgow Caledonian University, Child Poverty Resource Unit/Save the Children 1995*

Lone parents Scotland 1991 by gender and dependent children

Percentage of all lone parent households headed by:

Male lone parents	7.2
Female lone parents	92.8

Female lone parents as percentage of all lone parents with:

Children aged 0-4	96.3
Children aged 5-15	89.7
Children ages 0-4 and 5-15	96.7

Lone parents Scotland 1991 by economic activity

Employment status	% of lone parents
Full-time employed	15.5
Part-time employed	14.8
Self-employed	1.6
Government scheme/unemployed	7.9
Student	0.2
Economically inactive	60.0

Source: 1991 Census Scotland

Routes into parenthood (UK)

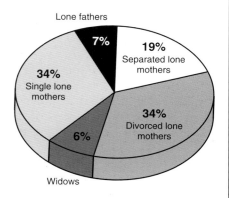

Lone fathers 7%
Separated lone mothers 19%
Divorced lone mothers 34%
Widows 6%
Single lone mothers 34%

Source: Population Trends 1993, HMSO

Lilley lone parent row revived

Minister rejects Bottomley's soft line on family rifts

By David Brindle
Social Services Correspondent

Photo: David Giles / Press Association

Peter Lilley, Social Security Secretary

Cabinet divisions over family policy flared into the open last night when Peter Lilley, the Social Security Secretary, publicly contradicted the benign stance towards lone parents taken by Virginia Bottomley, Health Secretary and minister responsible for family issues.

In a speech dwelling conspicuously on trends which Mrs Bottomley has sought to play down, Mr Lilley described the growth of family disruption as 'deeply disturbing' and claimed it was causing serious social and personal problems which could not be ignored.

His address, to a summer school at Birmingham cathedral, was also remarkable for an acknowledgement that the pay of unskilled workers has fallen so far in relative terms that they can barely take home more in wages than they would otherwise receive on benefit.

Blaming the fall on mechanisation, as opposed to government policy, he said the changing pattern of earnings was 'the main economic factor which may have affected the stability of marriage for some people'.

Mr Lilley, one of the Cabinet's rightwing minority facing a further squeeze in the pending reshuffle, has taken a low profile in recent months. During the European elections campaign, the Euro-sceptic minister spent more than a week at his holiday home in France and then campaigned in strong Labour seats.

His return to prominence last night will not endear him to the Prime Minister, who has been striving to play down the lone-parent issue since the controversy last autumn caused by the leaking of a Cabinet Office briefing paper on possible punitive measures against the 1.3 million one-parent families, about a million of whom live on benefit.

In Mrs Bottomley's first main address on family policy four weeks ago she took issue with the 'family pessimist' view linking divorce, births outside marriage and working women with crime and social decay.

Praising the parenting skills of most lone parents, she said it was not the size or nature of the family unit that mattered, but the long-term commitment given to raising the child. Mr Lilley, who describes himself as being on the Catholic wing of the Anglican church, told the summer school the divorce rate was alarmingly high and that the proportion of births outside marriage – 'indeed any stable union between the parents' – had risen even more dramatically.

'As a result of divorce, separation and illegitimacy, some 2 million children are brought up by a lone parent and some half-a-million families are step-families. Violence between men and women is a growing concern.

'The physical and sexual abuse of children, particularly involving household members who are not the natural parent, is an even more disturbing phenomenon.'

Most children, 'even from broken homes', did not become criminals, drug addicts or misfits. 'But there manifestly are serious and personal problems arising from the disruption of family life. We cannot ignore them. Nor should we.'

In what may be taken as a sideswipe at the creation of Mrs Bottomley's family policy role, Mr Lilley said it was a profound mistake to assume the Government had power to restore families to harmony or impose family values. One area where the state could exert long-term influence, however, was in helping people gain more skills to escape the jobs where pay had fallen in relative value.

With mechanisation 'unskilled young men cannot bring home a great deal more than the level of benefit. And some unskilled women cannot earn a great deal more in work than the benefits they would receive to enable them to bring up a child.'

The answer was certainly not to impose a minimum wage, but to do what the Government was already doing and reform comprehensively the schools and colleges, workplace training and the benefits system. 'It will take a generation to come to full fruition. But it is well under way,' Mr Lilley said.

In a speech for the Social Market Foundation last night, the former chancellor, Lord Lawson, echoed Mr Lilley's remarks when he said wages might be in danger of being pushed down so far they would 'involve levels of pay for the least skilled that a fundamentally wealthy society would consider too low to be acceptable'.

© *The Guardian*
June, 1995

In the name of the fathers

Single dads speak out

By Toby Harnden

Bob Huggins is no ordinary dad. Since his wife left him six years ago, he has raised three young children singlehanded, becoming something of a local celebrity in the process. 'I'm seen as an oddity. I hear the mums whispering: "There's that bloke who looks after the kids on his own",' Huggins says. 'My ex-wife thought I'd last two or three months and then give up.'

Last year Huggins was made redundant and he now cares for his children with the money he receives from Income Support and maintenance. After 33 years of work, he decided he had 'another job to do... one hell of a challenge.'

One in five families in Britain is headed by a lone parent. Fewer than one in 50 of these is male, although the numbers have been rising steadily: there were 70,000 lone father families in 1970 and 110,000 by 1990. Men have been coaxed into greater involvement in the 'female' domain of childrearing and the corollary has been that fathers are no longer prepared to accept that, in the event of a split, the mother should auto- matically look after their children.

According to single father Richard Egerton-Smith, the attitude of the 'divorce professionals' is simple: 'You're a man, you leave and then you pay up.' It took over a year after his wife left the marital home for him to be awarded care of his children, David, 11, and Alice, eight.

He can consider him- self lucky. John Latimer spent four years and made over 40 court appearances trying to prove that he could be a responsible single parent. The first judge, Latimer says, told him 'a woman has special qualities as regards children . . .They should be with their mother, and granted his ex-wife custody. The legal battle that ensued proved both costly and stressful. 'It's taken a toll on me but it has definitely been worth, it,' he says now. His two daughters, Yasmin, 17, and Kate, 13, have refused to see their mother during the four years since their father finally won custody.

> ### One in five families in Britain is headed by a lone parent. Fewer than one in 50 of these is male

It is often said that single fathers get more support than their female counterparts – Andrew Roff admits

Photo: David Gibson/Photofusion

to finding some mothers 'rushed to help me get my children on the bus' – and certainly they tend to do better in material terms. Dr John Haskey of the Office of Population Censuses and Surveys has found that single fathers are generally older, more likely to be working and, on average, earn more money than single mothers. Almost all have formerly been married; for single mothers, the proportion is about seven in every ten.

Practically, however, men who suddenly find themselves single fathers are often at a complete loss. From an early age, they have been conditioned to provide rather than to nurture. 'You don't know where to go or what to do when you're left alone,' Egerton-Smith says of a role for which he felt ill-prepared. Men are taught to be strong and self-reliant. They are not able to fall back on the informal system of mutual support so often available to women and are less ready to turn to others for help for fear of being branded 'unable to cope'.

On a national level, there is currently no organ- isation exclusively for single fathers, though local self-help groups are spring-ing up. Egerton-Smith was lucky: he spotted a news-paper advertisement that led him to Kingston-upon-Thames Single Dads' Support. It has a modest membership of 25 fathers, who meet at each other's homes to swap stories and advice.

Many of the obstacles placed in the way of single fathers are emotional rather than practical. The pressure to conform to gender stereotypes within the model of a traditional nuclear family is strong. In the latest British Social Attitudes' survey, 30 per cent of those questioned thought a single mother could bring up a child as well as a couple – only 23 per cent thought a single father could cope as well. Whereas mothers who look after children full-time are fulfilling the expected female role, men are seen as denying their masculinity.

When Andrew Roff gave up work to look after his four children, he encountered thinly disguised hostility from some. In the end, he says, 'I had to tell them: "I can understand what you're thinking but

---

Many of the obstacles placed in the way of single fathers are emotional rather than practical

---

no, I am not sexually abusing my children".'

For divorced single fathers, the fear that their ex-wife will seek custody is a potent one. Lawyers and court welfare officers (the majority of whom are women) are much more

likely to side with the mother, according to Egerton-Smith. 'It's just plain prejudice,' he says.

'It is difficult being Mum and Dad 24 hours a day,' Bob Huggins says. He believes 'the female side of men comes out a little bit' and that this is no bad thing.

For Huggins, who has just turned 50, there has only ever been one choice and that is to be with his children. What if his ex-wife had gained custody? 'That would have destroyed me,' he says simply. 'I would not have survived.'

© *The Guardian*
August, 1994

Bottomley speaks up for lone parents

There never was a golden age of the family and those who seek to blame social decay on its decline are wrong, Virginia Bottomley, the Health Secretary and minister for family policy, declared last night.

The proportion of families headed by a lone parent is 'not dissimilar' to that just before the first World War, the minister said in a key speech distancing her from cabinet colleagues and pundits who have linked social ills with the absence of a father from a household.

'We are too quick to condemn a minority of parents; too slow to praise that great majority of parents who discharge their responsibilities well,' Mrs Bottomley said.

Her comments came days after a fresh intervention by Charles Murray, an American social scientist who has strongly influenced those in Britain pinpointing the growing number of children born outside marriage as an indicator of social malaise.

Mr Murray forecasts that the trend will continue to spiral among poorer social groups, whom he terms the 'new rabble', while the middle

- The number of children in local authority care has fallen to about half that in 1980, an official report on implementation of the Children Act showed yesterday.

- There were 52,000 children being 'looked after' by local authorities in 1993, compared with 54,400 in 1992 and almost 60,000 in 1991.

classes will rediscover Victorian values.

Mrs Bottomley said she rejected the view that the family had never been under greater pressure because of births to unmarried mothers, now running at about a third of the total, and a divorce rate of one marriage in three.

Although the divorce rate was high, Britain also had the second-highest marriage rate in Europe and proportionally more people were married than at the turn of the century.

'The family pessimist view relies heavily on the notion that there was only a golden age of the family – that view is misguided,' said the minister.

Mrs Bottomley acknowledged that a married, two-parent family was the preferred environment for raising children. But she said most lone parents, many of whom did not choose to be without a partner, provided good care for their children – irrespective of poverty, disadvantage and adversity.

She also defended working mothers from accusations that they are a cause of family breakdown. About 70 per cent of married women go out to work, compared with 10 per cent in the 1930s.

'Some people distrust these developments. They refer to the "latch-key kid" argument. But do we really want to retreat to the days when many women were economically oppressed into unhappy relationships?' asked Mrs Bottomley, who was giving the annual lecture sponsored by *Community Care* magazine.

© *The Guardian*
May, 1994

'I was so terribly worried when she decided to keep the child'

The words 'teenage pregnancy' and 'irresponsible freeloader' are synonymous in the minds of politicians and members of the public. But often the reality is different. It is Granny, not the state, who steps into the breach. Maureen Freely talks to mothers who have coped with their daughters' pregnancies

It is almost every mother's secret dread. Just as the nest is beginning to empty, just as you're planning more time for yourself, your teenage, unmarried daughter comes home to tell you she's pregnant. You want to do the right thing, of course. But what does that mean? You don't want her weighed down with a baby. You want her to have a normal adolescence. But if she has a termination, will she suffer emotionally? If she has the child, will she even know how to look after it? Will her boyfriend support her? How will her father react? If the answer is 'badly', you may have to take sides. And if anything goes wrong, you are the one who will have to pick up the pieces.

When a teenage girl becomes a mother, who's really left holding the baby? Our politicians and leader writers claim it's the girl herself. More often than not, they say, her pregnancy is a ploy to help her jump the queue for a council flat – and spend the next 18 years undermining family values at the expense of the state. As the debate rages on, we have developed a nightmare image of this dangerous trouble-maker. She's the purple-haired, leather jacketed creature in Sainsbury's who slaps her toddler every time he asks a question. She's the waif with the Walkman and the killer Alsatian who spends her Child Benefit at the off-licence. She has thousands of faces, but she's never our daughter. When it happens to our daughter,

we don't have time to worry about the fabric of society. We just want to protect her.

Diana is a teacher in her mid-40s who lives outside Durham. Her husband is a VAT inspector. They have, in her words, a 'very happy family – three lovely daughters and a wonderful son'. About six years ago, she converted to Catholicism. Although her family appeared to respect her decision, she now thinks there were hidden tensions, 'because that was when it all started'. Her eldest daughter is 'a very nice girl, terribly sensible, but Harriet, my second . . .well, she's always been the more experimental type'.

'I consider myself very lucky. Not many women my age have the chance to bring up another child'

One afternoon not long after Harriet's 16th birthday, Diana was cleaning up her bedroom when she came across a Pill packet. 'I was horrified. Harriet is not a Catholic, but I still felt it was my duty to confront her. She had a new boyfriend. He had been pressurising her. I advised her to take it slowly. She threw away the pills and we left it at that. Three months later, she was

pregnant. I was so surprised – when we agreed to stop the Pill, I assumed she knew enough to stop having sex.

'The next thing I knew, she wanted a termination. My husband and I were very unhappy about that and eventually we persuaded her to have the baby, promising to look after her financially. She did book a termination, but she didn't go through with it. We were very pleased about that. She stayed with us, and I went all out to support her. I didn't go to the birth classes but I went along with her to the labour ward. She found the baby difficult at first but over time she's gained in confidence.

'When I think back on it, that first year was trying for all of us. Now Harriet lives in what used to be called our granny flat, but in the beginning she was in her old bedroom. This made it harder for her to make the jump from child to mother. Roland was a colicky baby for the first six months, and this did play on our nerves. Our main concern was for Harriet to do her A-levels. She wants to be a teacher and when Roland was 6 months old, she started at a sixth-form college not far from our home.

'It fell to me to organise the childcare. This was a headache, I must admit. I didn't want to begin with a childminder, as I do believe very strongly that a baby deserves individual attention, but we went through few nannies who turned out to be quite unsuitable. Eventually our cleaner took pity on us. She's a wonderful woman in her 50s with grown-up children. She looks after Roland in her house. I drop him off every morning on my way to work. It is a bit of a expense which has meant that we have have to economise on holidays. 'I suppose I ought to have let Harriet take more responsibility but my husband and I were afraid she might let inertia set in. She' a clever girl, but easily distracted, though I think she'll make an excellent teacher. 'We're always very nice to the boyfriend. He comes round quite a lot. He has a job now, and he's just finishing his course. It's looking as if they might get married. I've done a lot of the minding in the evenings, but I knew that would be the case. I'm an active grandparent. I got a few looks at the beginning, but I see no reason why I should be embarrassed. Because at least my daughter didn't have a termination. And I care about that.'

Ann has a quite different outlook to Diana. 'It's all very well for affluent, educated people in work to lecture us on morality. But the fact is, babies can ruin lives. And when my Susan came home with her news, the life that was going to get ruined most was mine.'

Ann is a mature student at a university in the Midlands. Her husband used to run a small construction business but it became one of the first casualties of the recession. 'He still gets odd jobs from time to time, but I started on my course with the idea of bringing a more reliable income into the family.' She's done much better than she expected to and is clearly enjoying her new life.

She was in her first year when 17 year old Susan, her eldest, 'came into the house one afternoon looking rather strange. Rather like Joan of Arc, I remember thinking. It was just as I was clearing up the tea that she dropped the bombshell. She just came out with it: "I'm having a baby and I'm going to keep it." At first I thought she was having me on. But she had it all worked out. She was going to leave school and get a place of her own. She had looked into the benefits. She was not going to involve her boyfriend. He had, in her words, "nothing to do with it," although she

did concede, after some rather unfriendly probing on my part, that he was the father. She had even gone and booked herself in with our GP! She continued floating around on this cloud for a fortnight.

'I can tell you it was the worst fortnight of my life. I can't describe the fury I felt at this poor girl. I'm quite ashamed of it now. After all those years of picking up after her, and her brother and sister, and their father, I was finally doing something for myself. My mind was opening. I was making my own friends. And now, with this crisis, I saw these open doors slamming in my face. It was almost as if she was doing this deliberately to keep me shut out!

If I had had the smallest indication that she understood the enormity of the task that she was undertaking, I might have felt differently. But I know my Susan. She's a romantic soul. I knew she would go out there and try and then, when she broke down, she would bring the pieces home to me.

Eventually I was able to convince her. We went back to our GP, who was very understanding. I don't think either of us has ever looked back. I can't pretend that I wasn't thinking of myself, but I have never doubted that a termination was the only feasible choice at the time for my daughter. She wouldn't have had a life. I think this was brought home to me vividly because most of the people on my course were not much older than Susan was at the time.'

What do mothers who themselves had babies very young think when their own teenage daughters get pregnant? Mary, now in her 40s, has never stopped regretting her early pregnancy. She was a 15 year old Cork schoolgirl when she had her son. She had been sent to Dublin to stay with relatives for the birth. When she came home, her mother took over the care of the baby. 'He knew I was his mother, but I could never call him mine.' This was and continues to be a source of great unhappiness. 'I know that I ended up setting up house with the wrong man just to prove to myself that I could cope without my mother. I would never put a daughter of mine through the same agony.' So when her own daughter became pregnant two years ago, she convinced her to put the child up for adoption.

'She took a year off school, then, after the birth in August, she went back to do her A-levels. She did very well, and she's now at Oxford. I'm happy to see her thriving. She seems to have put it all behind her. She leads a normal life. But I wonder if I do. Every once in a while it hits me: somewhere out there, I have a grandson.'

While probably no mother would want her single teenage daughter to fall pregnant, Stella says her entire family has benefited from the experience. The wife of a well-known artist, and mother of two, she admits money and a stable family background have helped enormously.

Her daughter Lottie was 18 when she got pregnant. 'After a lot of thought, she decided to keep the baby. I made it clear I would support her whatever her decision. The father wasn't around; I was the one with her at the birth. Lottie and the baby lived with me in Scotland for a month. After that, they moved out to a cottage nearby and Lottie got a job. I looked after Becca in the day and baby-sat in the evenings. I thought it was incredibly important that Lottie should have a life of her own.'

When Becca was 3, Lottie got a job in London, and so Stella and her husband moved with her. Although this sounds like a grand and generous gesture to the outsider, Stella describes it as the easiest, most natural thing in the world. It is as if she felt so bonded to Lottie and Becca that even to consider her own needs would have overtaxed her imagination. It is also clear that this time was a very happy one, not just for Stella, but for Stella's husband, who didn't seem to mind travelling and entertaining less. They lived together for four years. Just before I spoke to Stella, Lottie and Becca moved out. 'It's early days. They're renting a furnished flat not far from here. I still collect Becca from school, and then Lottie picks her up on her way home. Then I have her two evenings a week. I was so dreading their leaving, but actually it was all right. I have a bit of extra space and extra time, and I'm beginning to remember all the things that I quite enjoyed that I haven't even thought of doing for years. And Lottie and Becca are only up the road.

'My daughter has worked hard for her independence and I want her to enjoy it. Even with a helpful granny around, single motherhood is hard. If you're bringing up a child with its father, you can complain together without seeming disloyal. But if the other "parent" is your mother, you can't do that. 'I was so terribly worried in the beginning, when Lottie decided to keep the child. Incredibly anxious. Then Becca was born, and she was just a child you love. When they talk about single parents, what the children lack is money and family. But Becca hasn't lacked for either.

'I now consider myself very lucky. Not many women my age have the chance to bring up another child. I'll tell you what the nicest thing is about being the mother of a single parent – you're the only grandmother. You have no rival.'

Pregnancy rates in girls 19 and under

Great Britain (conceptions/1,000)	
England	64.8
N. Ireland	figures not available
Scotland (Source: Scottish Office)	48.4
Wales (Source: Office of Population Censuses and Surveys)	70.4

England by region

North Western (Lancashire)	79.2
W Midlands (Shropshire, Staffordshire, Birmingham)	74.0
Yorkshire (Hull, Leeds, York)	73.0
Northern (Cumbria, Northeast)	72.5
NE Thames (Essex, North and Central London)	69.3
Mersey (Liverpool, Wirral, Cheshire)	69.2
Trent (Derbyshire, Lincolnshire, South Yorkshire)	68.5
South East Thames (Sussex, Kent and S and E London)	63.3
Wessex (Dorset, Avon. Wiltshire)	55.1
NW Thames (Bedfordshire, Hertfordshire, W London)	54.9
East Anglia (Cambridge, Norwich)	53.9
Oxford (Berkshire, Northants, Oxfordshire)	51.8
SW Thames (Surrey, Hampshire)	48.3

Around the world (Births/1,000 among 15-19 year olds)

USA	53.6
England/Wales	33.2
Australia	26.5
Canada	23.2
West Germany	8.6
Holland	6.8
Japan	4.1

Source: Macro International Surveys

Sex and the under 16s	

Qualitative research carried out by Dr Colin Francombe of Middlesex University on under-age mothers.
(Based on a sample of 128)

How girls live

At home with parents	72.2%
Supported by partner	13.9%
With partner	9.5%
Hostel	2.4%
On benefits	44.9%
Supported by family	39.4%

Why girls first had sex

In love	59.7%
Curiosity	28.2%
Peer pressure	13.7%
Drunk	11.3%
Partner pressure	7.3%

Why precautions weren't taken

Had sex unexpectedly	65.4%
Thought it was illegal for GPs to give birth control to under 16s	43%
Thought GP would tell parents	38%
Didn't know about contraceptives or where to get them	28.4%
Didn't like to talk about it with boy	14.8%
Feared boy would leave if sex refused	4.9%
Age of boy – older	90%
Average age – boy	18.2
Average age – girl	14.5

Why three into sixteen won't go

The teenager pregnant with her third child embodies a social problem of our times. Elizabeth Grice asks the two sides of the benefits argument for their solution

She may not see it that way, but Dawn Hendy is a social disaster. She is 16, with two children and a third due in March. She and her boyfriend live in a two-bedroom council house in Mid-Glamorgan on benefits of £100 a week, which will increase after the birth of the third baby.

Dawn tells the world brightly she had no regrets about becoming a mother at the age of 14, no guilt about claiming benefits and every expectation that the council will rehouse her in a larger place before the latest child is born. Despite a spectacular failure with the contraceptive pill, she confidently declares that the new baby will be their last.

Fortunately for her two daughters, Alleisha and Charmaine, she loves being a mother and is probably even rather good at it. Unlike many other teenage mothers, her unemployed teenage boyfriend, Mike Carey, is living with her and shares the cleaning, cooking and nappy-changing. He would like to get a job. Happily again, the couple hope to get married. They are frugal with the housekeeping and don't find it a particular struggle to manage on £100 a week. 'We see ourselves as a family, just like any other couple,' Mike says.

Perhaps the most telling thing about their situation – premature parenthood apart – is that they are almost justified in thinking of themselves as a normal family unit. They are part of a cast of thousands for whom there is no stigma, no shame, and, as they see it, no alternative. If Dawn and Mike were 26 and 29 instead of 16 and 19, they would scarcely be noticed in the mass of parents bringing up children outside marriage, courtesy of the state.

The assurance with which she projects her future – 'by the time I'm 30 the children will be grown up and my life will be just beginning' – makes Dawn unusual. No one wishes her to fail. But her situation is such a failure of education, of expectation, of contraception and of incentive that it has plunged the Right and the Left of the political spectrum back into the long tunnel of the babies-on-benefit controversy.

The Right-wing solution, as propounded by Dr Digby Anderson of the Social Affairs Unit, is to withdraw state funds from feckless parents in the hope that it will encourage more responsible parenthood. He would like to see a return to mother-and-baby homes for single mothers, with encouragement to place children who could not be supported by their parents for adoption.

Dr Anderson does not believe in calculated babies-on-benefit. Very few young people, he argues, decide to have babies because they know they will be found council accommodation. The influences are more insidious and have to do with the way single parents are helped – and therefore assumed – to manage. 'By lowering the obstacles to single parenthood – they seemed to be doing all right, she got into a flat, the baby looked rather sweet – you lower the perceived obstacles. It is time to rebuild some sort of financial disincentives and stigma. But there is no way of doing that without hurting people. That is why politicians have not faced up to it, even though it would be worth it in the long run.'

Like Charles Murray, the American Right-wing political analyst, Dr Anderson believes that fractured families have children who are more likely than those from united families to be involved in crime, truancy and failure at school. But he agrees that the balance between compassion and the need to entice people into more responsible ways is fine.

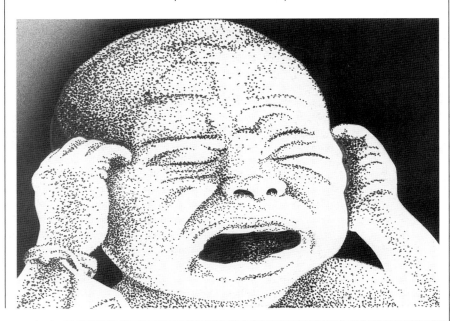

Mr Murray proposes that all benefits to new single mothers should be axed with nine months' notice. Single young women, he says, get pregnant because sex is fun and babies are endearing. He and his disciples are not persuaded that high unemployment is a good enough additional reason. 'If there is nothing you can do about unemployment, then it is responsible to say: "I will not have a child". That is a wrenching decision, but it is part and parcel of being a responsible adult.'

Dr Anderson supports in principle the New Jersey experiment of freeing state support for single mothers after a certain date, with proper notice. 'It announces that society is not going to encourage this way of life. It will not work in a week or a year but it is a declaration of intent.'

Malcolm Wicks, Labour MP for Croydon NW and former director of the Family Policy Studies Centre, represents the lobby that believes better sex education, better economic prospects and training for parenthood are the ways to help stem the state's expenditure on single-parent families. In 1991 there were 103,271 teenage conceptions. 'I do not think there is anything inevitable about this. The paradox is that this is the know-it-all generation but also a deeply ignorant generation.'

He agrees that the growing number of young single mothers is one of the most urgent problems facing the Government – by 2000 only half the nation's children will have a conventional family life, being brought up by parents who are married when their children are born and stay married until they grow up – but does not believe that withdrawing benefits is the answer.

'People are not living the life of Reilly on income support. They are mostly in grotty housing which is not heated properly. They live appalling lives in the worst housing in tower blocks on sink estates… Reducing the level of support will only make matters worse. What would stopping benefit mean? There are mad Republicans in the States talking about opening up orphanages again. That is simply not on.'

'We should be talking to young mothers about employment, education, training and trying to raise their self-confidence. And in boys as well as girls we have got to foster the idea of taking more seriously the business of being a parent.

'A lot of these mothers are victims of family breakdown. Any notion of cutting benefits and sending them back home to the loving arms of mum and dad is nonsense. The sort of agenda that could help us break out of this cycle must be about prevention and counselling, law reform that focuses on children and measures to enhance economic well-being.'

In 1979 there were 870,000 lone parents, only a third of whom were dependent on welfare. By 1991 there were 1.3 million, three-quarters claiming state support. For at least 15 years politicians have seen the looming problem but failed to stem the tide of dependency because they are afraid of being engulfed by the electoral consequences. Meanwhile, Dawn Hendy shows no such reluctance to improve her circumstances, whatever else may be on offer: she is in the process of selling her 'story'.

© The Telegraph plc
January, 1995

When motherhood means missed opportunities

By Peter White

Of the babies born in the world today, 20 per cent have a teenage mother. That's 15 million teenage births a year – of which 80 per cent are in the Third World. In parts of Latin America, 30 per cent of women give birth before the age of 20. In some African states, the figure is as high as 50 per cent. The USA has the highest rate of teenage pregnancy in the industrialised world, with a fifth of women giving birth before their twentieth birthday.

UNICEF, the United Nations Children's Fund, is concerned about these figures. It describes as 'staggering' the potential for even more teenage pregnancies and sexually transmitted diseases – not surprising given that there are some 500 million 15 to 19 year olds in the world today, most of them sexually active.

Early births reduce young women's opportunities in life. And their repercussions affect whole communities through disease, child and mother mortality, poverty and population growth.

Many of the causes of early pregnancies lie in a complex cycle of young women's low social status and little economic power.

But UNICEF believes that young people can be part of the solution. 'A girls' cycle of poverty must be replaced with a cycle of opportunity based on empowerment, legal protection, improved health services, expanded education and job opportunities,' it says.

How this might happen, and the changes necessary to bring it about, are spelled out in a well-illustrated colourful booklet, available free. For copies of *Too old for toys, too young for motherhood*, contact the information department at the UK Committee for UNICEF, 55 Lincoln's Inn Fields, London WC2A 3NB. Tel: 0171 405 5592.

© Young People Now
March 1995

The difficulties of setting up home for young single mothers

Young single mothers often find themselves catapulted simultaneously into independent adulthood and motherhood. Furthermore, many must come to terms with their new role and endeavour to establish an independent home quickly and with limited family support. Research by Newcastle University identified the following main problems for young mothers establishing a secure and suitable home for themselves and their children.

From 1971-91 the number of lone parents in Britain rose from 380,000 to 1,040,000, discounting lone fathers and widows. One group, lone unmarried mothers, has grown faster than any other, rising from 15.8 per cent of all lone parents in 1971 to 33 per cent in 1991.

Attention has focused recently on teenage unmarried mothers. However, births outside marriage to teenage single women have fallen as a percentage of all births outside marriage, from 34 per cent in 1979 to 22 per cent in 1990. What has increased is the likelihood of such births resulting in single lone motherhood, rather than 'shot-gun' weddings or co-habitation. As a result, there are more young single women with children trying to set up home.

The hunt for housing

Young mothers interviewed for the study still saw the local authority as the major provider of housing and knew little about other forms of tenure. Deposits, advance rents and landlords' attitudes all put them off private rented housing. They were suspicious of housing associations, believing that they did not offer the same security of tenure as local authority tenancies. Mothers were also wary of the higher rents paid for some housing association properties, even though the rent would be covered by housing benefit in almost all cases.

Mothers' priority in looking for housing was to be near their own family for support. However, available social housing in the study region is heavily concentrated in difficult-to-let areas. A mother wishing to remain in, or move to, a 'better' area will have to spend months or years on the waiting list. This makes it difficult for mothers to improve their circumstances as their needs change.

Extended periods in often overcrowded situations in the family home sometimes lead to the breakdown of family support and result in threatened or actual homelessness. The report found little evidence of homelessness being 'engineered' to speed up the housing process; women coming forward as homeless or threatened with homelessness were genuinely under great stress.

Those women accepted as homeless and allocated housing compromised their standards and preferences in order to be housed quickly; they were generally dissatisfied with their housing. Their dissatisfaction stemmed more from the social problems of the area than the condition of the actual property. One mother interviewed had overlooked the social problems of an area in order to remain near her own family in the first instance, but now finds herself trapped there long after her initial need for support has been replaced by that for a safer neighbourhood.

Furnishing the home

Despite the ready availability of local authority furnished tenancies in Newcastle, very few women knew of this as an option; those who did, did not find it attractive as they believed it tied them to second-rate, rented furniture for the duration of the tenancy. Some mothers feared they would be left having to pay the increased rent if they ever lost entitlement to housing benefit. Most women experienced great difficulty in furnishing a home, even to a minimum standard. Most had to compromise between doing without, buying poor quality, which would last only a short time, or going into debt. The majority set up home without adequate laundry facilities, seating, a fridge, a table, or a telephone and some remained without these facilities for many months or years. Few ever acquired a telephone (see Table 1).

Often the smaller household items such as bedding and

Table 1	Mothers without basic furniture and equipment N = 31	
	Initially	At interview
Bed (self)	7	1
Bed/cot (child)	5	1
Sofa/chairs	14	1
Table	27	16
Cooker	4	0
Fridge	17	8
Washing machine	21	10
Dryer	25	22
Television	6	2
Phone	26	23
Carpets (bedrooms)	22	8
Carpet (living rooms)	9	1
Vacuum cleaner	11	1

kitchenware proved most difficult to obtain or afford.

'Oh sheets me!... I'd love another pair of sheets ... I've only got the one pair so when I wash them I have to get them dry right that day ... If it rains I have to iron them dry...'

Even those mothers who had the support of their families could take little in the way of furniture from the family home or expect little in the way of financial help, most families already being stretched to the limit. The Social Fund was commonly felt to be either failing to help those in greatest need or offering loans which put already insufficient income under greater strain. Eighteen applied for a Social Fund loan, but only 8 were successful. Loan amounts seriously underestimated the real cost of furnishing a home. The study calculated that furnishing a home to the most basic minimum standard, not including carpet, would cost approximately £640 from second-hand shops or nearly £1,400 from the cheapest local retailers. Of the eight successful loan applicants, all but two received less than £500. The lowest amount was £147 offered to a young mother trying to furnish an entire home.

'You have to fight for everything, every single penny... Where else can you get money from?... It's not as if you're going to pay it back, is it?'

Many mothers did not apply for fear of not being able to cope with the repayments. Mothers often resorted to other forms of credit, such as catalogues and check traders, which are more expensive in the long run but have much lower weekly payments.

Preparing for a baby

Mothers receive £100 maternity allowance towards the cost of baby equipment. However, the most essential equipment – including a cot, a pram or pushchair and basic bedding, feeding and sterilising equipment – costs £499 from a basic range at Mothercare. A simple first set of baby clothing cost almost £60 at the cheapest market stalls in the study area. Mothers interviewed often received little in the way of

Photo: Sean Sprague / Panos Pictures

Once a mother and child are living alone, there is virtually no support available to them

gifts of baby clothing, the birth of an 'illegitimate' child not being seen as cause for such celebration.

'I thought it would be right after a while... they'd get used to the idea, be happy for me. But nobody said "Oh that's great", nobody said "congratulations". Only my Mam, in the end she came round bought us things for the bairn. You'd have thought someone was dying, not being born.'

Making ends meet

The vast majority of young single mothers were dependent on Income Support. Having a higher percentage of children under school age than other lone mothers they have a greater need of childcare. Their young age means they have little in the way of work experience to help them gain employment. They are also less likely to receive maintenance, so the combination of part-time earnings, Family Credit and maintenance is a less viable option. Income Support is age related with the youngest and most vulnerable women receiving the least financial assistance (see Table 2). The majority of mothers managed their finances extremely well; however, they frequently went

without themselves in order to provide well for their children. The average weekly amount spent on food and housekeeping by a mother with one child was £19. Many had to borrow regularly from friends or family just to survive on a weekly basis, others relied on eating at other people's houses. Independence can be put under great strain when this level of support from family and friends is not available.

'...I had to borrow off my Nan just to catch up. Now I owe her and she can't afford it neither... nobody's got no money in my family like... they'd help if they could.'

Asked how much they felt Income Support should be increased by, most felt that an additional £10.00 per week would make a real difference.

Mothers were ingenious in their attempts to stretch their incomes, robbing Peter to pay Paul and juggling gas and electricity payments to maximise their weekly benefits. However, when unforeseen expenses cropped up, such as the need to repair a washing machine, mothers often had to turn to credit leading to debt. In such cases, the Social Fund is of little

Table 2	Total weekly income for a single mother and one child from Income Support and Child Benefit	
16 and 17 years at home		£56.05
16-18 years living alone		£64.40
18 years and over at home or alone		£73.60

assistance. Mothers almost always turned to catalogues or other credit to meet expenses such as Christmas, birthdays or extra winter clothing.

Support and assistance

Young single mothers received little in the way of support and assistance. Many had limited contact with their families. Available support was spread between different agencies across the area; no one agency offered a young mother all the information and practical assistance she required in the initial days of setting up home. Many mothers gained their knowledge of the housing and benefit system from their peers.

Once a mother and child are living alone, there is virtually no support available to them. Youth, social and health workers are all limited in their ability to offer the intensive, on-going assistance mothers often need, especially if family support is not available. Those voluntary and community organisations which aim to support mothers and lone parents tend not to appeal to these younger women who feel 'out of place' amongst women even a few years older in their twenties.

In the more rural settings the voluntary sector has made few inroads and support is even more limited.

'There's not a lot of young mums round here, not as young as me anyway and they mostly have blokes. People look at you funny . . .'

Conclusions

Social policy does not distinguish between the different sub-groups of lone parents and does not recognise the additional needs and difficulties of this group, especially in trying to establish an independent home. The researchers conclude that:

● The problem has often been how best to reach these often isolated and self-conscious young women. There is an urgent need for the development of a multi-agency approach to assisting young single mothers in their efforts to establish and maintain an independent home. With almost every young mother approaching the local housing department, this need might be best met by the introduction of 'housing welfare officers' who would draw together all aspects of housing, health, youth and voluntary work to develop a co-ordinated plan for the housing and support of young single mothers.

● Voluntary agencies and community bodies aiming to support families under strain must identify and address the more specific needs of this group so as not to alienate them from the existing support networks of older women.

● Funding should be given to providers of supported accommodation to enable them to undertake intensive outreach support once a young single mother leaves the hostel.

The Joseph Rowntree Foundation is an independent, non-political body which funds programmes of research and innovative development in the fields of housing, social care and social policy. It publishes its findings rapidly and widely so that they can inform current debate and practice.

● The above is a summary of the report *The difficulties of setting up home for young single mothers* published by the Joseph Rowntree Foundation. See page 39 for address details.

© *Joseph Rowntree Foundation*

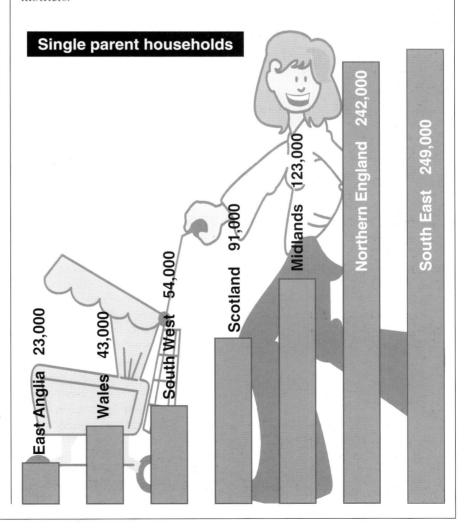

Single parent households

East Anglia 23,000
Wales 43,000
South West 54,000
Scotland 91,000
Midlands 123,000
Northern England 242,000
South East 249,000

Teenage pregnancy

Introduction

The conception rate for all teenagers rose from 56 conceptions per 1,000 women in 1983 to 69 conceptions per 1,000 women in 1990. This figure fell to 65.1 in 1991.[1] The number of conceptions to younger teenagers has been increasing. One of the targets set by the *Health of the Nation* is to reduce the rate of conceptions amongst the under 16s from the 1989 figure of 9.5 per 1,000 girls aged 13-15 to no more than 4.8 by the year 2000.[2]

In 1992, some 48,000 teenagers in England and Wales had a baby,[3] about 7 per cent of all births. These figures are a slight reduction on those for the 1980s. The current teenage fertility rate is 32 births per 1,000 women aged 15-19, a much lower figure than the peak of 51 in 1971.

Teenage abortions have risen during the last 20 years and rates of conception leading to abortion rose from 14.3 conceptions per 1000 teenage women in 1971 to 24.6 by 1990.[1]

Today, fewer teenagers marry but many cohabit. In 1991, 83 per cent of teenage mothers were single, against the figure of 30 per cent for mothers of all ages. In 1961 only 20 per cent of teenage mothers were single. Marrying when pregnant is commoner among teenagers compared to other age groups. In 1990 nearly one in four teenage brides was pregnant on her wedding day compared with one in ten older brides. However, of those remaining single, three-quarters register the birth jointly with the baby's father, and the great majority of these couples are cohabiting.[1]

Geographical and social variation

Rates of teenage conception, abortion and childbirth show considerable variation among Regional Health Authority areas.[1,4]

Local studies in Glasgow,[5] Tayside[6] and the North East Thames Region[7] report a strong association between areas of low socio-economic status and both high teenage pregnancy rates and a low proportion of teenage pregnancies which end in abortion. Teenage motherhood remains predominantly a working-class experience.[1,8,9]

Teenage sexual behaviour

Evidence over the past 30 years suggests that teenagers are having their first sexual experience at ever younger ages, although the threat of AIDS may be slowing or even halting this trend. Numbers of those having their first intercourse before 16 have increased: currently about one in four teenage men and one in six teenage women. Around half of 16 year olds and around 80 per cent of 19 year olds are now sexually experienced.[9-12] Working-class boys, but not girls, are likely to begin at younger ages than their middle-class peers.[9,13]

Premarital sex appears to be condoned by almost all teenagers, although most disapprove of extramarital sex.[9] Most adolescent sexual activity takes place within steady relationships, although there is a significant level of infidelity within such relationships, and fairly frequent changes of partner. Almost half of all male teenagers and a quarter of females condoned sex with someone who was not a steady partner.[11]

Among sexually active teenagers, the Pill remains the commonest contraceptive technique, used by about two in five. One in three uses condoms. However, about a quarter use no contraception[14,15] and that figure is higher among those not in a regular relationship, or with several partners. Condom use appears to decline, and Pill use to increase, as couples enter steady relationships. The belief that it becomes no longer necessary to use a condom with a steady partner, and its impact on pleasure, are the main reasons for condom non-use.[14] Contraceptive use among teenage girls who become teenage mothers is low, and among very young teenage mothers, almost non-existent. Many are unsure how to obtain contraceptives.[8,16-18] Some appear to have given up reliable techniques without any clear desire to become pregnant.[8]

Attitudes towards pregnancy and motherhood

Measuring changes in attitude is beyond the scope of most research, but some attempts have been made to find out what teenagers feel about their pregnancy. Phoenix[16] divides her sample into those who wanted to conceive (22 per cent); those who did not mind either way (25 per cent); those who had not considered the possibility of pregnancy (18 per cent); and those who had thought it important to conceive when they did (35 per cent). Earlier research with a sample of 102 young women in Bristol found that 28 per cent had planned the pregnancy; 10 per cent were ambivalent; 16 per cent had not planned it but were pleased at the news; and 46 per cent had neither planned the pregnancy nor were pleased at the news.[8] Younger teenagers are especially likely to enter into pregnancy without considering the consequences of their actions. [15, 19] Phoenix notes that by late pregnancy the feelings of both teenagers and those close to them had become more positive.[16] The reasons why teenagers carry their pregnancy to term, despite initial fears and unpromising circumstances, are many and varied. Ignorance or denial of the pregnancy; teenage rebellion; a desire for adult status; or the need for an object to love, are some of the 18 reasons listed by Hudson and Ineichen.[8]

The under-16s

The conception rate among 13 to 15 year olds increased steadily from 6.8/1,000 in 1969 to 10.1/1,000 in 1990, but fell back in 1991 to 9.3. Roughly half of all conceptions to this age-group are aborted.[1]

Young women having first sexual intercourse under the age of 16 are the least likely to use contraception.[10] They are the least likely in their sexual activity to be aware of the risks, to seek contraceptive advice, to get advice when sought, and to use advice effectively when received. Concern about confidentiality, which has been a major deterrent in seeking advice, is now being addressed.[20] They are the least likely to be in a stable relationship, whilst still the most in need of parenting, and the least able to envisage realistically the consequences of bringing up a child.

Although legally, financially and emotionally dependent on her parents, a girl under 16 may usually choose the outcome of her pregnancy. However the High Court reserves the right to make the final decision on the basis of the girl's best interests. Decision-making is especially problematic for such young women, who may receive conflicting messages from the putative father, friends, relatives, professionals and the media.

Among sexually active teenagers, the Pill remains the commonest contraceptive technique, used by about two in five, one in three uses condoms. However, about a quarter use no contraception.

Once she proceeds towards motherhood, she may claim free milk tokens and dental care, and on her 16th birthday Income Support in her own right regardless of her parents' economic status. The £100 maternity grant is available only at 16 or under 16 if the girl's parents are on Income Support or Family Credit. Regardless of age, all parents receive Child Benefit.

Educationally, many of those who become pregnant very young, and opt for motherhood, experience difficulty in continuing at school. Many are poor attenders prior to the pregnancy; some have been out of school for a year or more.[23] With no national policy on the education of schoolgirl mothers, provision is patchy in the different LEAs.[21] Few are able to go to college, into training or to find employment, due to restricted public funds,[22] reduced grants, poor training schemes, lack of relevant qualifications, poor self-esteem, lack of confidence, but above all lack of childcare.[8] Gribben describes a programme designed to equip teenage mothers with basic parenting skills.[23]

Health

The health of teenage mothers has often been described as poorer than that of older mothers, and particularly poor for younger teenage mothers. However, a large recent study in Hull found few differences in health between pregnant younger teenagers and pregnant women in their early 20s. Exceptions were anaemia, urinary tract infections and hypertension, all commoner in the younger group.[17] Smoking and drinking patterns may be relatively heavy in pregnant teenagers.[8] Emotional disturbance may also be common, especially if the decision about whether or not to seek an abortion is a difficult one.[24] Teenagers may through their ineffective use of contraception find themselves vulnerable to AIDS and other sexually transmitted diseases.[8,13,25,26] Diet may be poor and the use of health services patchy. Teenage mothers are less likely to breastfeed their children.[27]

Outcome

Longitudinal studies from Britain and America are revealing that, while the initial disadvantages of pregnant teenagers and their offspring (which are financial and occupational as well as social and familial) persist throughout their adult years, poor outcomes are by no means inevitable. Many teenage mothers and their children achieve good levels of educational and occupational progress.[28]

Confusing policies

While the need for increasing provision of contraceptive services for young people is widely admitted, no central source of funding is available. GPs are urged to target young people requiring contraceptive advice, but are offered no significant financial incentives to do so.

The recent amendment to the Education Act 1993 makes sex education compulsory in secondary schools from September 1994, but allows parents to withdraw their children, and removes human sexual behaviour and its effects on HIV/AIDS infection from the National Curriculum in Science. Additionally, government spending on health education co-ordinators has been cut, leaving Britain with the highest teenage fertility rates in Europe.[1]

The needs of teenagers

The Health of the Nation targets[2] challenge the insufficient provision of sex education and health services to Britain's children and adolescents. It is widely felt that sex education should be professionalised and take place in schools.[29] Such a move often leads to safer sexual practices and sometimes to a delay or decrease in sexual activity. In none of the 19 studies in one review[30] was sex education found to lead to earlier or increased sexual activity. The threat of AIDS makes effective protection essential. Clinics providing contraceptive advice and counselling need to be accessible, confidential and user-friendly for adolescents of both sexes.[29] Specially trained health visitors have been shown to be valuable in reducing the risk of child abuse by teenage parents.[31]

Boys need particular help, and should be brought into decision-making around contraception. Young women need encouragement to be more assertive in their sexual relationships[32] and offered a greater prospect of further education, vocational training and meaningful jobs. Reliable childcare is essential.[38] A recently published directory lists residential provision, educational facilities, including parenthood education, and support and advice agencies for pregnant teenagers and young parents throughout Britain.[39]

Much can be learnt from abroad. The Netherlands in particular boasts a very low teenage pregnancy rate due to broader, more open social attitudes, a generous approach to sex education in schools and contraceptive services widely available to young people.[33-35] In America some bold innovations in the provision of school-based clinics have dramatically reduced the number of adolescent pregnancies.[36, 37]

References

1   Babb, P (1993) Teenage conceptions and fertility in England and Wales 1971-91, *Population Trends*, 74, 12-7
2   Department of Health (1992) *The health of the nation.* HMSO
3   OPCS (1993) *Population Trends,* 74
4   Wilson, S H et al (1992) Teenage conception and contraception in the English regions, *Journal of Public Health Medicine* 14, 1, 17-25
5   Rosenberg, K and McEwan, H P (1991) Teenage pregnancy in Scotland: trends and risks, *Scottish Medical Journal* 36, 172-4
6   Smith, T (1993) Influence of socio-economic factors on attaining targets for reducing teenage pregnancies, *British Medical Journal* 306, 6887, 1232-5
7   Garlick, R et al (1993) The UPA score and teenage pregnancy, *Public Health* 107, 135-9
8   Hudson, F and Ineichen, B (1991) *Taking it lying down: sexuality and teenage motherhood.* Macmillan
9   Wellings, K et al (1994) *Sexual Behaviour in Britain.* Penguin
10 Johnson, A M et al (1994) *Sexual attitudes and lifestyles.* Blackwell
11 Ford, N (1993) *The sexual and contraceptive life-styles of young people.* Part 1 *British Journal of Family Planning* 18, 52-5
12 Breakwell, G M and Fife-Scraw, C (1992) Sexual activities and preferences in a United Kingdom sample of 16 to 20-year-olds, *Archives of Sexual Behaviour* 21, 3, 271-293
13 Bury, J (1991) Teenage sexual behaviour and the impact of AIDS, *Health Education Journal* 50, 1, 43-9
14 Ford, N (1993) The sexual and contraceptive life-styles of young people Part 2, *British Journal of Family Planning* 18, 119-22
15 Mellanby, A et al (1993) Teenagers, sex and risk-taking, *British Medical Journal* 307, 6895, 25
16 Phoenix, A (1991) *Young Mothers?* Polity
17 Konje J C et al (1992) Early teenage pregnancies in Hull, *British Journal of Obstetrics and Gynaecology* 99, 969-73
18 Family Planning Association (1993) *Children who have children*
19 Munday, K et al (1993) Why teenagers get pregnant, *Primary Health Care*, 3, 5, 12-13
20 Scally, G (1993) Confidentiality, contraception and young people, *British Medical Journal* 307, 6913, 1157-8
21 Dawson, N (1989) Report on the 1987 survey of educational provision for pregnant schoolgirls and schoolgirl mothers, *Journal of Adolescent Health and Welfare* 2,1, 7-8
22 Field, F (1989) *Losing out: the emergence of Britain's underclass.* Blackwell
23 Gribben, M (1992) *Seeking out the wounded child* Barnardo's
24 Maskey, S (1991) Teenage pregnancy: doubts, incentives, and psychiatric disturbances, *Journal of the Royal Society of Medicine* 84, 723-5
25 Mellanby, A et al (1992) Teenagers and the risk of STDs: a need for the provision of balanced information, *Genito-Urinary Medicine* 68, 4, 241-4
26 Baron, C and Butler, A eds (1992) HIV/AIDS *and sex education for young people.* All-Party Parliamentary Group on AIDS
27 OPCS (1992) *Infant feeding 1990.* HMSO
28 Lawson, A and Rhode, D L eds (1993) *The politics of pregnancy: adolescent pregnancy and public policy.* Yale University Press
29 Allen, 1 (1991) *Family planning and pregnancy counselling projects for young people.* Policy Studies Institute
30 Barth, R P et al (1992) Preventing adolescent pregnancy with social and cognitive skills, *Journal of Adolescent Research* 2, 208-32
31 Early Childhood Development Unit, University of Bristol (1992) *Child protection: the impact of the child development programme*
32 Lees, S (1993) *Sugar and spice: sexuality and teenage girls.* Penguin
33 Wardle, S A and Wright, P I (1993) Family planning services: the needs of young people: a report from Mid-Staffordshire, *British Journal of Family Planning* 19, 158-60
34 Nyman, V (1993) Going Dutch: a pipe dream? *British Journal of Family Planning* 19, 200-3
35 Clark, A and Searle, E S (1994) Flying Dutch visit: lessons for the UK on sex education and abortion, *British Journal of Sexual Medicine* Jan/Feb, 4-5
36 Keenan, T (1986) School-based adolescent health care services, *Paediatric Nursing* 12, 5, 365-9
37 Miller, B C et al, eds (1992) *Preventing adolescent pregnancy.* Sage
38 Norman, C and Wilks, S (1993) *A fit state for motherhood?* Children's Society
39 Di Salvo, P and Skuse, T (1993) *The really helpful directory.* Trust for the Study of Adolescence/Maternity Alliance Bernard Ineichen and Frances Hudson

● The above is **Highlight No.126**, written by Bernard Ineichen and Frances Hudson and produced by the Library and Information Service at the National Children's Bureau. See page 39 for address details.

The autonomous female

A young unmarried mother tells Margarette Driscoll that she is better off living without a man

Angela Foster is typical of a generation of independent single mothers for whom a man is an option rather than a necessity. She has a five-year-old daughter, Lulu, and lives in Birmingham.

Lulu's father left when Angela was a few weeks pregnant and returned just before the birth. They had an on-off relationship that finally ended 18 months ago. Angela never felt dependent on him; they lived in her house and she was the one who worked.

'On one level it was ingrained in me that I would meet a guy, fall in love and play happy families, but I was also brought up to believe I was equal, that the world was my oyster, and the two just don't mix,' she said.

'I always knew that if I had a child I would be totally responsible. That is always the case. The mother has the bottom-line responsibility for the children even in a marriage. The difference is that now you don't need a man to validate your existence.'

She believes the reason so many women have rejected men is less to do with finance than attitude. Men have not been able to adapt to new working patterns and resent women for usurping their role.

'Men haven't come round to the idea that women want to do more than fetch and carry for them. We have moved from manufacturing to the computer and they can't cope. They don't have the self-respect brought by work and they haven't got it in the family because we don't need them.'

As time goes on there will be fewer and fewer eligible men to go round

---

Until recently, when she opened a shop with the help of the enterprise allowance scheme, Angela was dependent on benefits. She now pays herself £65 a week, which is topped up by £55.50 family credit. She is about £10 a week worse off working than she was on benefit, but considerably better off than she might have been had she married a man without a decently paid job.

As time goes on there will be fewer and fewer eligible men to go round. Two-thirds of women now work compared with half in the 1970s. By the end of the century it is forecast that women will make up a majority of the workforce. A man with no role is a drain, both on financial and emotional resources.

'Too many of them still think the world owes them a living. They don't have the same get-on-with-it attitude as women,' Angela said.

'We have the motivation and the expectations now. Men seem to be content to sit around chewing the fat about what a hard time they are having. A friend's boyfriend was made redundant a while back and she said, 'Why don't you get a job in a bar?' He was horrified. He thought it was beneath him.

'That's typical, I've waitressed, I've worked in bars, worked 72 hours a week doing hard physical graft. I know lots of single mothers and they are all trying to better themselves. They are the ones who take college courses, do the retraining schemes.

'Men still want you to be at home doing the cooking, even if they contribute nothing, and they won't do the housework themselves.

'I can't take the idea of men seriously as "providers". I don't want a man who can pay for me. It would be nice to find one who could pay for himself.'

© *The Sunday Times* *November, 1994*

What they need is a home

Young single mothers – and their housing – will be much in the headlines this week. Christina Hardyment puts forward a novel solution to halt a growing problem

It is a modern myth, and one that took hold quickly and surprisingly completely; that the typical single mothers is a feckless teenager who deliberately became pregnant to jump the council housing queue.

This week that myth – and indeed the legion of young, single mothers themselves – will be much discussed and dissected. Already in the High Court is the action between the BBC and the Broadcasting Complaints Commission, centring on a *Panorama* programme of last year.

Panorama looked at a council estate in South Wales and came down very much on the side of The Myth; they filmed girls who had indeed become mothers to escape the restrictions of life with parents or boyfriends and to acquire a home of their own. The National Council For One Parent Families complained; and the Broadcasting Complaints Commission upheld its complaint. Hence the High Court action.

If the case had been held up just a few days, the QCs engaged might have had a solid basis of research over which to argue. For the end of this week will see the publication of an extraordinarily comprehensive report on the present state of the family. The roll call of the great and the good summoned by the Joseph Rowntree Foundation to assist in its preparation reads like a New Year's honours list. From Left, Right and Centre, learned opinions have been heard and duly recorded.

As the report's cumbersome title *Family and parenthood: supporting families, preventing breakdown* suggests, there are no simple nostrums that are going to transform us into the cornflake packet families that were, we fondly believe, standard issue in the Fifties. It is under-standably wary of conclusions; it says that we must accept the new realities and tailor piecemeal solutions to fit the many different situations that confront families in a rapidly evolving society.

The suggestions are un-doubtedly well meaning, but surely what is needed is a far simpler, more immediately understand-able set of rules to govern the desperately serious game of creating new lives. Suppose that it was made clear that all homeless expectant mothers would be housed not in a home of their own, but a Home with a capital H? Young women need to accept that having a baby is not a right that is automatically subsidised, but a privilege to be earned. It is a suggestion that needs discussion.

On the plus side, it appears from the report that things are not nearly as bad as we sometimes believe. Eighty per cent of children under the age if 16 live with both their natural parents. Half of all divorces concern couples whose children have left home or who are childless. Most cohabitation ends in marriage.

But shuffling statistics to make our cup of domestic happiness seem half full rather than half empty is not to say that everything in the garden is rosy. There has been a real deterioration in the financial circum-stances of families as opposed to singles or childless couples. Even relatively well-off families are finding that it takes two, or at least one-and-a-half, salaries to keep themselves in the style to which their parents were accustomed.

'The favourable direct taxation treatment of working parents with children that existed 30 years ago has been eroded under successive governments,' says David Utting, the report's compiler.

Economic strains are putting pressure on relationships, and divorces, especially among families with small children, are once again on the up. The report also admits that the fastest growing new trend is the increasing proportion of families headed by single, never-married mums – up from 1 per cent in 1971 to 7 per cent in 1991, although it points out that an unknown number are ex-cohabitees who might more properly be classified under the same heading as separated or divorced mothers (now 11 per cent of families).

It points to the huge pressure on housing that so many broken homes create, but refutes the idea that teenage mums are jumping the queue for council housing. A report by the Institute of Housing could find no local authorities which gave prece-dence of this sort. The realities facing indigent young single mums are very different. To get anywhere at all, they have to be officially homeless, and once nominally housed, their lot is more likely to be lumpy mattresses in bed and breakfasts than feather-bedding on benefits.

A disproportionate number then occupy small flats in rundown estates where children may actually outnumber adults, with disastrous consequences in terms of delinquency. A Catch-22 'poverty plateau' means that earning up to £170 a week loses a single mum so many benefits that she is only £13 a week better off than if she stays at home and lives on Family Credit.

The problem is that, although The Myth may be just that, a myth, it is believed as much by young girls as by hard-Right backbenchers. Very few young women considering motherhood are going to read the small print of this report – which is why the suggestion of a new generation of what were once known as Homes for Fallen Women makes sense. They would both dispel the myth and tackle the problems many young mothers face.

I know how difficult things really are. I think the support – and the company – I get here is marvellous.

The homes would be supportive rather than penal; a friendly, maternal sorority providing a base from which mothers could further their education or train for a job. They could remain until their children were old enough for nursery school or they had other means of support.

We already have a well-tried basis on which to build. Today, a perinatal stay at a small mother and baby home often proves to be an effective way for lonely and stressed young mothers to learn the basics of babycare and to establish friendships and contacts that provide a support network later on. But girls are expected to move on when the baby is about six months old, and then many fall on hard times.

'But young girls don't want to live in homes and hostels,' comes the cry. 'They want to set up their own homes.'

'Very young mums may well feel that,' says Angela, 34, who was only too happy to find a place with five other single mums in an Oxford home for young expectant mothers run by the charity Life.

'I've been through all the hassle of living in a rundown bed and breakfast room and of trying to find anything halfway decent in the way of accommodation. I know how difficult things really are. I think the support – and the company – I get here is marvellous. And there's follow-up when we leave.'

Homes for unsupported mums (Hums?) could well concentrate the minds of young girls wonderfully.

© *The Telegraph Plc*
February, 1995

Housing

Locating sources of support

Many young single mothers feel isolated and out of place. They do not have access to adequate support, especially when faced, as many are, with the need to set up an independent home quickly and without much help from family.

So say researchers from Newcastle University in a report into the main problems young mothers face in establishing a secure and suitable home for themselves and their children.

One of the chief findings of the survey of young, never married mothers who had given birth to their first child as a teenager was that no one agency offered all the information and practical help needed in the early days of setting up a home.

Many mothers learnt about the housing and benefit system from their peers. Their age made many feel alienated and 'out of place' with voluntary support groups among mothers just a few years older. 'There's not a lot of young mums round here. Not as young as me anyway, and they mostly have blokes,' said one young women. 'People look at you funny . . .'

Young mothers saw the local authority as the main provider of housing, and knew little about other forms of rented accommodation.

'Deposits, advance rents and landlords' attitudes all put them off private rented housing' say the researchers. 'They were suspicious of housing associations, believing that they did not offer the same security of tenure as local authority tenancies.'

Many of the young mothers surveyed had limited contact with their families. Once a mother and child are living alone there is virtually no support for them. Youth, social and health workers are limited in their ability to offer the intensive, ongoing support often needed. The report concludes that there is an urgent need for a multi-agency approach to assist young single mothers. One suggestion is that this could be provided by housing welfare officers based at the agency that almost all young mothers approached – the local housing department.

● A summary of the report *The difficulties of setting up home for young single mothers* is published by the Joseph Rowntree Foundation as Social Policy Research Findings No. 72. See page 39 for address details.

© *Young People Now*
May, 1995

Households and families

The proportion of teenage girls (aged 13 to 19) becoming pregnant fell sharply in the 1970s, but started rising again in the early 1980s and in 1990 there were 69 conceptions per thousand teenage women in England and Wales. In 1991 teenage pregnancies fell sharply to 65 conceptions per thousand 15 to 19 year olds, but it is too early to tell if this indicates a change in trend. The rate for under 16s was 9 conception per thousand girls aged 13 to 15 in 1991 and reducing this is one of the *Health of the nation* targets. The target for England implies a rate of 4.8 conceptions per thousand girls under 16 in the year 2000. About half those who conceived before they were 16 had an abortion in 1991. For older teenagers maternities outnumbered abortions', and altogether two-thirds of teenagers who conceived had the baby.

Unmarried teenagers becoming pregnant are far less likely to get married than 20 years ago. In 1971 one in three pregnant unmarried teenagers had their baby inside marriage compared to 1 in 11 in 1991.

TEENAGE CONCEPTION RATES: BY TYPE OF AREA, 1991

England and Wales (Rate per 1,000 women)	All conceptions		Leading to maternities	
	Aged under 16[1]	Aged under 20[2]	Aged under 16[1]	Aged under 20[2]
Inner London	12.5	90.4	6.3	51.1
Principal cities	13.3	83.2	7.5	68.4
Other metropolitan districts	12.2	79.1	6.5	55.9
Other cities	12.4	76.6	6.9	54.1
Industrial non-metropolitan districts	10.7	72.1	5.4	50.4
New towns	10.3	71.1	5.0	49.1
Outer London	7.2	59.9	3.2	33.3
Resort and retirement	7.8	59.1	3.5	37.9
Remoter largely rural	6.3	48.9	2.5	30.9
Mixed urban/rural	5.7	43.7	2.2	24.7
All areas	9.3	65.1	4.6	42.7

[1] As a proportion of girls aged 13-15. [2] As a proportion of girls aged 15-19. *Source: Office of Population Censuses and Surveys*

The youngest mothers

The experience of pregnancy and motherhood among young women of school age

The Youngest Mothers: The experience of pregnancy and motherhood among young women of school age.

By Gillian Schofield
Published by Avebury (1994)
£30:00, 137 pages
ISBN 185628 843 9

An often-cited health target, set out in the government's *Health of the nation* document (1992), is a reduction by 50 per cent of the rate of conceptions under the age of 16. Early teenage pregnancy is seen as a sign of the nation's sexual ill-health. Such pregnancies are invariably depicted as 'unwanted' – not even unintended – a medical problem rather than a social issue.

Pregnant 15 year olds, especially in media reporting, are often grouped with people suffering from AIDS and other sexually transmitted diseases. They are frequently subjected to an even wider range of negative images.

It must be acknowledged that such stereotypes can arise as a result of concern for what is deemed to be their plight; unfortunately, the effect is to reinforce the stigma and prejudice which fuel discriminatory attitudes.

Rarely does anyone listen to what these young mothers have to say about their own experiences; Schofield, in contrast, places the stories told by young mothers themselves at the very centre of her account of this often invisible and largely silent population.

Such stories are inevitably very mixed. Schofield draws on their experiences at each stage.

Pregnancy: the reactions of young women on discovering they were pregnant, the reactions of their families, the attitudes of the fathers, the responses of their schools – and

---

By Howard Williamson

---

particularly the value of the local tuition unit which offered a safe haven and more mature learning environment – and the attitudes of the medical profession. Birth: giving birth alone, with their mother present, and with their boyfriend present.

Here Schofield makes the significant point that, far from things being out of the ordinary because of the mother's age, things were 'essentially normal' in terms of the range of emotions expressed, 'all reminiscent of older mothers'.

Rarely does anyone listen to what these young mothers have to say about their own experiences

---

Motherhood: the mother's personal resources and resilience, the child, the family, the fathers. The two issues which are especially pertinent to these young women are that they invariably live at home

and that they are more likely to be in a position of having to care for the child on their own. Again, a mixed bag of perspectives emerges on these matters.

What is of great importance is the infrastructure of support available to them. These young women require advice, support, reassurance, a sense of belonging and security. They may wish to continue their education; they may wish to go to work.

They must feel that such choices and possibilities remain open to them and that the fact of young motherhood has not curtailed other pathways to adulthood. Indeed, a major contribution made by the tuition unit was to enable young mothers to take pride and pleasure in their babies while building their self-esteem as women.

After the richness of the young women's stories, Schofield's analysis of key themes and service recommendations appears somewhat bland. They do, of course, need to be outlined but they are implicit threads within the stories themselves – if we are listening to them properly.

The value lies in the challenge it provides to the prevailing negative portrayals of young mothers. Schofield presents a picture of activity, battling and survival, often – though certainly not always – in the face of disadvantage and adversity.

Early pregnancy clearly does confer significant obstacles on those young women who experience it, but their voices are not dejected or downtrodden.

As Schofield herself concludes, 'a sense of pride in what they have achieved, a sense of humour about their difficulties and a degree of wisdom about the pattern of their lives comes across very strongly'.

INDEX

ADDITIONAL RESOURCES

You might like to contact the following organisations for further information. Due to the increasing cost of postage, many organisations cannot respond to inquiries unless they receive a stamped, addressed envelope.

Campaign Against the Child Support Act (CACSA)
PO Box 287
London NW6 5QU
Tel: 0171 837 7509 (voice/minicom)
Fax: 0171 833 4817

Families Need Fathers
c/o BM Families
London WC1N 3XX
Tel: 0171 613 5060

Family and Youth Concern
322 Woodstock Road
Oxford OX2 7NS
Tel: 0865 568 48

Family Mediation Scotland
127 Rose Street
South Lane
Edinburgh EH2 4BB
Tel: 0131 220 1610
Fax: 0131 220 6895

Family Planning Association
27-35 Mortimer Street
London W1N 7RJ
Tel: 0171 636 7866

Family Policy Studies Centre
231 Baker Street
London NW1 6XE
Tel: 0171 486 8211

Describes and analyses family trends and consider their implications for public policy; to consider the impact of policies on families of different kinds.

Institute for Family Policy Research
30-32 Southampton Street
London WC2E 7RA
Tel: 0171 379 9400
Fax: 0171 497 0373

International Planned Parenthood Federation
Regents College
Regent's Park
London NW1 4NS
Tel: 0171 486 0741
Fax: 0171 487 7950

Joseph Rowntree Foundation
The Homestead
40 Water End
York YO3 6LP
Tel: 01904 629241
Fax: 01904 620072

The Foundation is an independent, non-political body which funds programmes of research and innovative development in the fields of housing, social care and social policy. It publishes its research findings rapidly and widely so that they can inform current debate and practice.

National Association of Family Mediation
Charitybase
The Chandlery
50 Westminster Bridge Road
London SE1 7QY
Tel: 0171 721 7658/7647
Fax: 0171 721 7643

National Child Birth Trust
Alexandra House
Oldham Terrace
London W3 6NH
Tel: 0181 992 8637

National Children's Bureau
8 Wakely Street
London EC1V 7QE
Tel: 0171 843 6000
Fax: 0171 843 6000

National Council for One Parent Families
255 Kentish Town Road
London NW5 2LX
Tel: 0171 267 1361
Fax: 0171 482 4851

A national inter-disciplinary organisation concerned with children's needs in the family, school and society.

National Youth Agency
17-23 Albion Street
Leicester LE1 6GD
Tel: 0116 2856789
Fax: 0116 2471043

Acts as an resource centre for youth work policy makers in the UK. Its major concerns include, informal personal and social education, employment, education, training initiatives and community involvement.

NCH Action for Children
85 Highbury Park
London N5 1UD
Tel: 0171 226 2033
Fax: 0171 226 2537

A child care charity with over 200 projects helping 16,000 children and young people each year.

Northern Ireland Family Mediation Service
76 Dublin Road
Belfast BT2 7HP
Tel: 01232 322914

One Parent Families Scotland
(previously the Scottish Council for Single Parents)
13 Gayfield Square
Edinburgh EH1 3NX
Tel: 0131 556 3899
Fax: 0131 557 9650

Scottish Child and Family Alliance
55 Albany Street
Edinburgh EH1 3QY
Tel: 0131 559 2780

United Nations International Year of the Family
c/o Family Policy Studies Centre
231 Baker Street
London NW1 6XE
Tel: 0171 486 8211

Women's Aid Federation England
PO Box 391
Bristol BS997WS
Tel: 0117 9633 494

ACKNOWLEDGEMENTS

The publisher is grateful for permission to reproduce the following material.

Chapter One: One-parent families

Lone parenthood, © The Family Policy Studies Centre, September 1994, *Lone mothers in Britain*, © OPCS, 1994, *Around the world*, © One Parent Families, Scotland, May 1995, *National Council for One-parent Families*, © National Council for One Parent Families, *Key facts*, © National Council for One Parent Families, March 1995, *When the cupboard is bare*, © The Family Policy Studies Centre, April 1995, *Poverty for children as parents go it alone*, © The Daily Mail, May 1995, *Are you missing out on £300 a year?*, © Today, January 1995, *One parent benefit*, © Department of Social security, *Lone parent link to poverty triggers MP's call for benefits reappraisal*, © The Guardian, March 1995, *Lone parents income*, © National Council for One Parent Families, March 1995, *On your own with a baby*, © One Parent Families, Scotland, April 1995, *The trials of a toddler with wanderlust*, © The Herald, March 1995, *Lone parents*, © Glasgow Caledonian University, Child Poverty Resource Unit, Save the Children, 1995, *Lilley lone parent row revived*, © The Guardian, June 1995, *In the name of the fathers*, © The Guardian, August 1994, *Bottomley speaks up for lone parents*, © The Guardian, May 1994.

Chapter Two: Young Single Parents

'I was terribly worried when she decided to keep the child', © Good Housekeeping, National Magazine Company Ltd, April 1995, *Pregnancy rates in girls 19 and under*, © Good Housekeeping, National Magazine Company Ltd, April 1995, *Why three into sixteen won't go*, © The Telegraph Plc, London 1995, *When motherhood means missed opportunities*, © Young People Now, March 1995, *The difficulties of setting up home for young single mothers*, © Joseph Rowntree Foundation, *Teenage pregnancy*, © National Children's Bureau, March 1994, *The autonomous female*, © The Sunday Times, November 1994, *What they need is a home*, © The Daily Telegraph, London 1995, *Housing*, © Young People Now, May 1995, *Households and families*, © HMSO Reproduced with the kind permission of Her Majesty's Stationery Office, 1995, *The youngest mothers*, Young People Now, June 1995.

Photographs and Illustrations

Pages 3, 17, 23: Emma Dodd/Folio Collective, page 4: Mo Wilson/Format, pages 7, 10, 33, 36: Andrew Smith/Folio Collective, page 19: David Giles/Press Association, page 20: David Gibson/Photofusion, pages 25, 30: Anthony Haythornthwaite/Folio Collective, page 28: Sean Sprague/Panos Pictures.

Craig Donnellan
Cambridge
September, 1995